THE PUB AND ENGLISH SOCIAL CHANGE

AMS STUDIES IN ANTHROPOLOGY: No. 4

ISSN 0738-064X

Series Editor: Robert J. Theodoratus
Department of Anthropology, Colorado State University

1. Christopher Boehm. *Montenegrin Social Organization and Values: Political Ethnography of a Refuge Area Tribal Adaptation.*
2. Paul Driben. *Aroland Is Our Home: An Incomplete Victory in Applied Anthropology.*
3. Janet Kestenberg Amighi. *The Zoroastrians of Iran: Conversion, Assimilation, or Persistence.*
4. Daniel E. Vasey. *The Pub and English Social Change.*
5. Juliene G. Lipson. *Jews for Jesus: An Anthropological Study.*
6. Bruce T. Williams. *Coal Dust in Their Blood: The Work and Lives of Underground Coal Miners.*
7. Gerhard H. W. Roggenkamp. *Germans and Gastarbeiter: A Study of Prejudice.*
8. George A. Boeck, Jr. *Texas Livestock Auctions: A Folklife Ethnography.*
9. Leopoldo José Bartolomé. *The Colonos of Apóstoles: Adaptive Strategy and Ethnicity in a Polish-Ukranian Settlement in Northeast Argentina.*

THE PUB AND ENGLISH
SOCIAL CHANGE

Daniel E. Vasey

AMS PRESS
New York

Library of Congress Cataloging-in-Publication Data

Vasey, Daniel E.
    The pub and English social change / Daniel E. Vasey.
        p.   cm. — (AMS studies in anthropology; no. 4)
    Bibliography: p.
    Includes index.
    ISBN 0-404-62604-1
    1. Hotels, taverns, etc. — England — History. 2. England — Social life and customs. 3. Drinking customs — England. I. Title. II. Series.
TX910.G7V37   1990
394.1'3'0942 — dc19   89-31180
                                                                          CIP

All AMS Books are printed on acid-free paper that meets the guidelines for performance and durability of the Committee on Production Guidelines for Book Longevity of the Council on Library Resources.

AMS Press, Inc.
56 East 13th Street
New York, N.Y. 10003

Manufactured in the United States of America

CONTENTS

FIGURES

TABLES

MAPS

ACKNOWLEDGEMENTS

Many people assisted in some way the original study, but special thanks are due to the dissertation committee chairperson, Carroll L. Riley, and committee members Edwin A. Cook, Basil Hedrick, Vernon Johnson, Joel M. Maring, and Jon D. Muller. Brewery spokesmen, who preferred to be anonymous, contributed valuable information, and the staff of the British Museum and the Cambridge University Library rendered assistance in many ways on countless occasions.

Robert J. Theodoratus, the general editor of this series, got the revision going and provided suggestions that benefited it greatly. I must also thank Greer S. Vasey, who was once a pub informant, and Natasha Vasey, who could not have been one, for their help preparing the manuscript.

Finally, a toast to the cast, all the pubgoers and publicans, those I crossed paths with and the many more I never met, for they have all contributed to something unique and wonderful, the English pub.

PREFACE

Three comments are most worth making regarding the sixteen years that have elapsed since the first writing of this report. For one, pubs have continued evolving in many of the directions that were apparent in 1970-71, but pub conservationists, who would preserve older styles, have organized themselves, particularly in the "real ale" movement, which involves more than just beer. Second, years of high unemployment superseded the period of rapidly rising incomes during which the observations were made, muting talk of affluence and embourgeoisement of the working class. Finally, systems models are less fashionable among human ecologists. Some would go so far as to deem passe discussions of equilibrium and change such as that found here in Chapters One and Five. It seems to me now that I anticipated and met the crucial objection that systems models are inherently static, but failed to do so with sufficient clarity. Therefore, I now endeavor to clarify without altering the original interpretation.

Much of the impression that systems models are static comes from the peculiar fascination of 1960s cultural ecologists with steady states and homeostasis. In reaction some social anthropologists and archaeologists have followed a path paved two decades or so ago by sociologists sailing in Talcott Parson's wake, namely, insisting that change is the normal social condition, or, in systems language, that positive feedback greatly outweighs negative feedback. A neat rhetorical stance, and irrefutable given the historical record, it makes of equilibrium and change a dichotomy that I find false now as much as at the first writing.

The great advantage of the systems model for this study is that it provides a framework in which to integrate social and environmental data without giving one or the other priority. The anthropologist might argue that the histories of pubs and other environments that are cultural artifacts are but facets of cultural histories, and they would be correct about final cause, but architectural historians have long found it useful to trace the evolution of things set in concrete. The original decision to synthesize pubs and pubgoers into pub systems was made for the parsimony that it gave to analysis and to comparison with trends in English society, but I would now add that such a synthesis is what human ecology should be.

THE STUDY OF BUILT ENVIRONMENTS AND THE METHODS OF THIS STUDY

Studies of design and the use of space have a long
history. Lewis Henry Morgan's <u>Houses and House-Life of the
American Aborigines</u> (1965, orig. 1881) a century ago broke
ground by relating cultural factors and social usage to the
design of built environments. The Chicago School of
Sociology earlier in this century fostered research in design
and society, though its focus was principally on larger
units, namely, cities and whole neighborhoods. More recently
Osmond (1957) and Sommer (1959, 1961, 1969) stimulated
interest in smaller built environments.

Sommer and his students and associates evolved an
experimental method intended to establish individual needs
for space and to identify social rules that govern spacing,
principally but not exclusively the distances that people
insert among themselves in various settings. Experiments
have been carried out in such environments as a library
(Russo 1969), schools (Norum, Russo and Sommer 1967), a jury
room (Strodtbeck and Hook 1961) and a college dormitory
(Sommer 1969).

A unifying concept of these researches is <u>personal space</u>
(Sommer 1959, 1969), that which a person takes up in a given

social context. Personal space is not just an individual
requirement, but also a message from one person to another.

Sommer (1969:5-6) acknowledges that the interaction
between environment and social use involves more than just
space. Noting that architects commonly rely on photographs
rather than texts to convey ideas, he adds that he makes a
point of showing "glossies" when addressing groups of
architects. All designers deal routinely with a complex set
of interactions among environments and their users.

Temperature, sound, color, odor and many other factors
are part of the designers' conception of space. Social
scientists must inevitably find it hard to convey in words
the gestalt of an environment, but can describe those
features of the environment and of behavior that are most
closely associated. The ethnographer of a public place can
also describe much behavior that is not apparent from
photographs, including much of personal interaction.

The approach of environmental psychologists such as
Sommer can provide useful perspectives on the history of
built environments, but does not by itself yield history, and
for that reason this study must diverge. When the task is to
describe the histories of pubs and pubgoers, the holism that
Sommer finds in architects is worth imitating as much as
possible. As many have noted, behavior, usage, and artifacts
of design tend to evolve in partially stereotyped
trajectories creating types that are widely recognized.

Cavan (1966) demonstrates that San Fransisco bars, because of distinctive physical features, tend to match up with types of clientele; most bargoers have made the same observation in less rigorous fashion. A certain type of establishment, say, a singles bar or a gay bar, is what it is because of its customers and because of its design and decor. A bar may be designed to attract particular patrons or may evolve with its clientele.

In England as in San Francisco pubs and pub clientele find one another so that everyone is suitably placed. A differences is that English pubs more often contain several rooms licensed for drinking, rooms that frequently vary greatly in clientele and design. A single room is sometimes divided into two distinct environments. This study accordingly associates pubgoers with pub settings more than with whole pubs. Each of the pub systems described in Chapter Five is a whole made up of culturally stereotyped environmental features and appropriate behavior, elements that are messages that integrate the system. These systems are fairly consistent throughout England, regional styles notwithstanding, but the types are not so rigid as to preclude inventiveness in the design and use of individual pub settings. The coherence of the systems justifies the use of the systems concept, whether or not formal systems theories are applied. The use of such theories is suggested because of their frequent application to other forms of

human-environmental interaction, albeit most often in very
different contexts.

A SYSTEMS MODEL

A "system," in its simplest meaning, is a whole made up
of integrated elements. The elements of pub systems include
people, actions, and objects. The inclusion of people and
their environments suggests a parallel with ecosystems, or
better, with cultural ecosystems (Geertz 1963), systems of
human-environmental interaction mediated by culture. Though
ecological anthropologists tend to focus on whole communities
and the niches they occupy in their environments, it is
recognized that the whole set of systems is hierarchical.
For example:

> Members of the process school [of archaeology] view
> human behavior as a point of overlap (or
> "articulation") between a vast number of systems, each
> of which encompasses both cultural and noncultural
> phenomena...(Flannery 1967:119).

A crucial difference between ecosystems and the systems
in this study is that the former are primarily maintained by
exchanges of energy, the latter by the transmission of
messages in the form of pub behavior and artifacts of the pub
environment. The aim of Chapter Five is to describe those
systems operant in pubs in which significant change is
evident, particularly by noting shifts in the relative
importance of these systems. Typologies of pub settings and
clientele, while a useful aid in the analysis, do not in

themselves lead to nearly so elegant a framework for
describing change as does the typology of systems. One
reason is that a given setting in a pub may be used in
different ways at different times, sometimes at the same
moment, and pubgoers as a matter of course take part in
several different types of pub environments, all the while
altering their behavior to match.

Systems Identity and Change

     Systems models are an ideal vehicle in which to deal with
pub systems that are variously old or relatively new, but
which hold many elements that turn over frequently. Formal
systems analysis shares the integrative aspects of
functionalism, but demands a dynamic historical approach
rather than a synchronic one. General systems theory,
cybernetics, information theory, classical market economics,
and the theory of games are all built on concepts of
equilibrium which embody constant change. An assumption
common to all these approaches is that internal mechanisms
operate to maintain equilibrium, tending to iron out
disturbances but not necessarily to produce stagnation; a
common misrepresentation of equilibrium is to confuse it with
a steady state in which long term change is nil, or with
homeostasis, exemplified by body temperature, in cybernetics
a condition of equilibrium regulated within tight limits.

Social systems inevitably change, due variously to changes in the external environment whose effects cannot be compensated or to changes that originate within the system itself, yet these changes take place alongside mechanisms that act to maintain the system's identity. In cybernetics and general systems theory the maintenance of system identity and of equilibrium are largely synonymous, and some theorists assume some form of equilibrium wherever the system appears to maintain some degree of stability over the long term, a proposition linked to certain assumptions of isomorphism among physical, biological, and social systems that are beyond the compass of this book. Equilibrium is most readily demonstrated in some measurable state, including some, such as population or the price of eggs, that are broadly social, but no such state is very meaningful within pub systems. I shall therefore seek only to demonstrate that pub systems too accomodate the maintenance of their identity to cumulative change, but not to demonstrate equilibrium in specific states of these systems. The oldest pub system, that which shall here be termed the "regulars' system," is a particularly appropriate example. Ever since Anglo-Saxon times a few cronies have gathered in the home of a neighbor who brews and sells beer, a custom reflected in the modern forms of address: "landlord" and "guest." The plans of those settings which today form the usual haunts of the regulars often echo those of the alehouse kitchen, the room in which all medieval

villagers, including those who brewed, played host. The
original alehouse kitchen has evolved, however, and
diversified. Among associated activities, table games have
remained a regulars' pastime for centuries, but the favored
games have turned over many times. One or two types of beer
predominate at any one time, but the specific favorites are
alway subject to the whims of fashion. For example, porter,
once the draught beer of London's workingmen, is today sold
in bottles, mostly to older women. Unity of the regulars
sometimes demands changing conventions of behavior. The
regulars' etiquette banning the discussion of politics was
dropped without ill effects during the era of working class
militancy in the late nineteenth century; presumably
solidarity won out over divisiveness.

Much that is appropriate to a system at one time later
becomes inappropriate, but participants always recognize the
continuing tradition. _Plus ca change_, _plus c'est la meme_
chose expresses the principle very well; the system becomes
established even as it evolves.

Messages and Systems

Individuals identify a system by reading appropriate
messages from the environment and from other participants.
Dark colors, rough textures, cribbage games and certain
manners of address all signal the regulars'system to some
extent, particularly when several such messages are read

together. The total perceived semantic value of the system
approximates the folk term "atmosphere" that abounds in
literature and talk about pubs. Especially striking is the
ability of experienced pubgoers to predict fairly accurately
the interior of a strange pub and many of the goings on
inside from a quick glance at the outside of the building.
Pubs exteriors display symbols with richly traditional
associations. Many are there by design. An iron lantern
over the door, plain facing, and a back street location are
sufficient though not necessary signs of a neighborhood
"local."

A pub system's smooth functioning requires that
participants have the appropriate perceptions, know the rules
in operation, and place the messages they receive in the
culturally proper perspective. The identity of the system,
more precisely its continuance in distinctive form, depends
upon the effective transmission of appropriate messages,
something equally apparent whether we speak of a system in
general or its manifestation in one place.

Critics of curent pub change frequently argue that the
loss of conventional artifacts is too great for traditional
usage and atmosphere, what I would call the outward
manifestations of systems, to absorb without becoming
something else. They fear imposed homogeneity, e.g.:

> ...is it necessary to plaster a house which had a
> degree of personality with the gimmickry of the image-
> creators' fantastic longing for uniformity (Morning
> Advertiser, The Times, June 17, 1971, p. 14)?

Trade representatives deny the accusation, countering that the traditional pub is alive, well, and if anything improved by its physical alteration. They thus differ with the critics over the indispensability of elements long associated with certain systems.

The pub study included an examination of this issue, particularly of the essentiality to the whole system of key elements said to affect atmosphere, clientele or usage. The method of study is historical and ethnographic and aims at a coherent analysis and presentation, but wholly intersubjective conclusions are probably not obtainable in this way.

CULTURAL CONTEXT AND "PROXEMICS"

Pub systems operate and evolve within a larger culture, so that all behavior associated with the houses is as English as it is "pubish." After Morgan, the pioneer student in anthropology of cultural differences in the use of space was Edward Hall (1959, 1963, 1966, 1968), who is especially concerned with communication by means of interpersonal spacing, and who coined "proxemics" for his particular method. Though this study made no use of proxemics; with its system of notation for posture, touch, voice loudness, and other variables of space and interaction; Hall's work reminds us that the norms and values of the whole culture color the meaning of behavior and of artifacts. A given feature common

to English pubs, American bars, and Greek <u>kafanas</u> might have
a different meaning in each. Beyond this, Hall's relativism
goes beyond what can be supported by this study:

> ...the principles laid down by Whorf and his followers
> in relation to language apply to all culturally
> patterned behavior, but particularly to the aspects of
> culture which are most often taken for granted and
> operate as Sapir (1927) so aptly put it- "in accordance
> with an elaborate and secret code that is written
> nowhere, known by none, and understood by all" (Hall
> 1968:84).

Certainly pub systems contain semantic elements that are
either uniquely English or are given a unique meaning in an
English setting, but to suggest a grammar that operates below
the surface of consciousness, one parallel in its
pervasiveness and perhaps its complexity to the grammar of a
natural language, goes far beyond the evidence. Informants
were sensitive to cues of environment and usage. Though I
could and did recast their concept of atmosphere into the
mold of historical system, I did not derive rules at a deeper
level to account for their behavior and their judgments.
Pubgoers are entirely capable of being both component and
critic of a pub system, whereas speakers of a language, in
every sentence they utter, obey a very large number of
grammatical rules, enough to forestall speech if they were in
the speakers' consciousnesses.

METHODS

Participant-observation was the principal field technique, one necessitated by the task of identifying complex, integrated systems. Only the combination of participation and observation would allow unity to be perceived from many disparate elements, but the breadth of the study added special methodological difficulties to the familiar one of accounting for the effect of the participant-observer.

Work in depth was not possible in a sizeable sample of the country's approximately 60,000 pubs. Geographical variation could not be completely taken into account. If a typical pub existed, sampling would not have been a concern, but the Tudor stereotype notwithstanding, no such thing ever became apparent.

All the problems of studying the culture of a complex society apply when the subject is the pub. The two most common approaches to the study of complex societies, apart from social survey methods of little applicability in this framework, are the "community-study" technique and the use of whatever statistical or other data can be gleaned for the whole society. The original intention was to combine these approaches, using each method as a control on the other.

In practice "community study" technique, as understood by most of its advocates, was partly sacrificed. Two towns were selected for special scrutiny, but were not so much studied

in their entirety as they were used as convenient and
contrasting clusters of pubs.

Bolton, Lancashire, a northern industrial town of
150,000, was chosen because Mass-Observation (1970) made a
detailed study of its pubs in the late 1930's, providing a
basis for comparison. Bolton's pubs were studied from
February to early June, 1971. Besides time spent in the
pubs, enquiry was made on the design and composition of
neighborhoods and on local government policy towards the
licensed trade. The other case needed to be a contrast.

Fenston, a pseudonym, is a southern (East Anglia) market
town of about 10,000 people. Work there, from October, 1970
to February, 1971 and again for three weeks in June, 1971
included more time outside the pubs than in Bolton.
Fenston's social and political structure was more accessible,
through informal interviews, and through such documentary
sources as town records, newspaper files, a directory of
associations and organizations, and some local histories and
private records. These sources are sufficient to add
valuable insights to the analysis of the Fenston pubs and to
allow comparison with the locales of more detailed English
community studies.

Nearly three months were spent traveling from pub to pub,
mainly in other parts of England, but also in Wales,
Scotland, and the Irish Republic. Particular attention was
paid to The City and East End of London, Manchester,

Newcastle-upon-Tyne, Cambridge, and to pubs in country

villages and large housing estates near Bolton and Fenston.

On a first visit I would concentrate on observation and

not join in unless invited, more the exception than the rule.

Receptivity was typically greatest in back street and country

houses and where the licensed room was small and intimate.

The hospitality of the Newcastle "Geordies" lived up to its

positive reputation. If more visits followed I was

invariably asked my purpose, to which I answered studying

pubs. Most accepted the explanation, though often with the

twist that I must be intending to open up an English style

pub in the United States. Until my purpose was well known

and accepted I usually took notes after I left. At times,

when breaking that rule where I was not well known, I was

taken for a bookie. On only one occasion did anyone take

apparent offence to my note taking.

Within the pubs were three intensities of observation,

all fairly natural categories with little overlapping. The

data from these categories were kept separate.

(1) Participant-observation as an accepted regular was

successfully carried out in 15 of Fenston's 18 pubs, and 18

of Bolton's 140, together comprising what will be referred

to as the primary sample. The Bolton pubs were drawn in

nine random pairs, coupled to reduce the time spent walking

between pubs. "Regular" covers a range of degrees of

establishment in the pub's life. In one Fenston pub I had

all the recognition and privileges of a long time regular
and played (badly) in a "friendly" darts match against an out
of town rival. I resided in this particular house for
one month. In another four houses I was an accepted fixture
and on good terms but not one of the inner circle, the
publican's old time associates. The larger average size of
Bolton pubs was an obstacle to gaining an equal degree of
acceptance, although I acquired "mates" at most in this
sample.

(2) A lesser total number of visits were made to
establish the weekly round of activities, sample the
clientele, and record the design, sales, and services of the
house. Ten was the average number of visits, but the range
was wide, depending on how readily the cycle of activity
became apparent. Each visit would last at least an hour. A
rough reading of the age, sex, and social class of the
clientele was usually possible. By rough I mean that age was
a careful guess, social class - "blue collar" or "white
collar" after the Registrar-General's classification -
something inferred from crude criteria, e.g., dialect and
working clothes. By way of comparison, in the pubs where I
attained regular's status (above), I generally knew the other
regulars' ages and occupations. Pubs in this secondary
sample included the remaining Fenston houses, twenty-four in
Bolton, several in villages and council estates (public
housing) near Fenston and Bolton, and several each in

Newcastle, Manchester, London (three in Bethnal Green), and Cambridge.

(3) A brief visit or two took in the design and services and sampled the clientele of the moment. Included were the remaining Bolton pubs and most of the houses visited on the road.

A sample of patrons of pubs in the primary sample were asked to respond to a questionnaire. The questions were asked verbally, and are given in Appendix Two, along with the sampling method.

Four of the twelve breweries approached for interviews responded. These were Greene and King, Greenall Whitley, Watney-Mann North, and a firm in the top six whose representatives did not wish to be identified. Discussions with managers of the tied (brewery owned) houses covered construction, renovation and design, the selection of tenants, product marketing, clubs within pubs, long term trends in the trade, and open ended responses to the topic of my research. Statistical sources, trade literature, and scholarly works, cited throughout the text, round out the sources of information.

Rapport came easily. This was no doubt partly due to my not being identified with any particular group. One person put it this way: "As an American, you are classless here." The judgement is accurate enough that I readily interacted with the less than law abiding fringes of society at a

everywhere accepted as a social equal, rather that I was
never a threat to anyone's status. I did not fit the one
most familiar role of a pubgoing American in either Fenston
or Bolton, namely that of military personnel from nearby
bases.

The perceived role of a pub researcher was not especially
detrimental. Some people felt I might be doing something
more productive, others that being on a fellowship while
quaffing beer was quite droll, but no one was particularly
concerned, no more than if I had been working at some unseen
job and coming to the pubs for recreation. Some part of the
ethnographer's actions in the field is unavoidably peculiar
by local standards, but people fortunately make allowances
for the behavior of outsiders.

One occupational hazard, the beer itself, undid a few
observations when I was not careful. I could not drink
nonalcoholic beverages without adversely affecting rapport,
first because it made me stand out, and second because many
individuals object to buying soft drinks when standing
rounds. When drinking in a group or expecting to do so, I
usually stuck to half pints of mild ale, a brew low enough in
alcohol that "mate" and clear headed ethnographer could be
one and the same. Etiquette makes it difficult though not
impossible to change drinks in midstream. The problem was
not serious, however, and on the whole the work went smoothly.

THE EVOLUTION OF THE PUB

Most communities have regular gathering places, and in
Europe houses serving beverages have had this function since the
classical civilizations. The drink often gives its name to the
place, as in mead hall, bierstube, kafana, cafe and others, and
by the middle ages entrepreneurs had established beverage houses
in towns and cities throughout Europe. Their commercial nature
sets them apart from many counterparts around the world. There
is ordinarily no formal means of member selection, no corporate
group of users. Nevertheless, the drinking houses are part of a
world wide phenomenon, whereby the men, at least, of a tribe,
village, or neighborhood gather gather around pots and cups of a
beverage.

ENGLISH DRINKING PLACES BEFORE 1830

In late medieval England drinking houses were established
as the main social centers, apart from homes and places of
work. Roman Britain had its wine taverns, and the Anglo-
Saxon epic Beowulf describes a mead hall. Beer, referring to
any beverage fermented from grain, was the main drink of
England from Saxon times on. The technical demands of
brewing must have favored the development of specialists who

made and sold beer. Household brewing was the rule among the
Saxons and fell to the wife as a domestic chore. The beer
was not hopped and kept but a few days. Brewing in large
batches was an obvious efficiency, so it is not surprising
that some people early started brewing for other households.
Throughout the Middle Ages beer was mostly sold to be taken
home, but premises also developed to accommodate the drinker.

The major task of this chapter is to trace the evolution
of the pub, in all its forms, from these early beginnings.
Interested readers are referred to a large literature on pub
history, including several more or less comprehensive
summaries (Askwith 1928; McGill 1969; Monckton 1968).

For a description of the main themes in pub design it is
hard to improve upon Gorham and Dunnett (1950:20). They
trace three main historical lines based mainly on design
criteria: (1) "home from home," with origins in the medieval
alehouse, (2) "grander than home," which arose from the
medieval inn, and (3) "frankly theatrical," which dates
mainly from the "gin palaces" of the Regency and early
Victorian periods. The types are not necessarily peculiar to
England or to places that serve beer; an interesting parallel
is to be found in a study of medieval Near East coffee
houses, which Hattox (1985) divides into "small, local
shops," strongly reminiscent of the alehouse, and "coffee
houses in the grand tradition," that from the description are
at least "grander than home," some "frankly theatrical."

Gorham and Dunnett's typology coincides fairly well with one based on social use, and it will be returned to with respect to modern pubs. Historically, "frankly theatrical" represents a fashion in design that eventually appears in houses with diverse social uses. "Home from home" and "frankly theatrical" are historically more essential and perhaps more consistent social forms, inasmuch as both lines are very old and yet still viable today. The tavern developed parallel to the alehouse, and the two always saw similar use, notwithstanding some significant differences in clientele. Taverns therefore have largely belonged to the home from home tradition, though their pretensions, which were usually at least a little grander than those of the alehouse, were sometimes enough to place them in the grander than home class.

Alehouses, Taverns and Coffee houses

The alehouse grew out of the brewer's home. Then as now people with simple homes normally entertained guests in the kitchen, which logically was also the usual room for serving beer. By Tudor times interior provisions had become fairly ample, and thereafter drinking rooms were commonly separate, but a pattern carried over from the cottage kitchen: a small, plain room with rough tables and benches centered on a hearth, conversation set at close quarters and foaming glasses of beer brought from cellar barrels by the hosts.

Signs let passersby know that a batch of beer was ready.
Although any stranger might enter, the alehouse remained
foremost a place where a neighborhood clientele collected, as
"guests" of the "host" in his home. A few village alehouses,
including some that are still standing, contained a number of
serving rooms and other elaborations, but in general
buildings on this order tended to be taverns, not alehouses.

Alehouses were found in towns and cities from the Saxon
era on, and their number increased steadily with the greater
prosperity of succeeding centuries. They do not seem to have
been prevalent in manorial villages until well after the
close of the Norman period (Lennard 1959:387), although
villeins as early as the twelfth century did sometimes brew
for sale, paying a tax in beer in return for the use of the
lord's implements (Monckton 1966:41). The number of
alehouses in proportion to the population reached a peak in
the seventeenth century and then steadily declined (Appendix
One). Many pubs today, particularly those in the country
villages and back streets, and more commonly in the south,
retain the form and function of the old alehouse, although
beer (only) licenses have declined sharply during the last
two decades.

The distinction between alehouse and tavern was always a
bit vague, even in contemporary accounts, but the latter was
generally distinguished by the provision of wine, later of
spirits, in addition to beer. With a more expensive stock in

trade, the taverns had a greater capitalization than the
alehouses and therefore a greater potential to reward
investment and elaboration. By and large, the potential was
realized. The question thus arises whether the clientele of
the two types of houses differed, a point on which opinions
differ.

Higher nobility remained sequestered in their manors, but
accounts tell of mixing of other levels of society in taverns
and alehouses. In Piers Plowman a cleric, a tart, a
gamekeeper and various artisans mix freely in a village
alehouse. References to common folk going to taverns are in
Homans (1965:299-300) and in Chaucer's Miller's Tale. A
number of later writers remarked similarly. Samuel Johnson's
accounts of his tavern clique, in the eighteenth century,
describe a great deal of social mixing. And in one old
verse:

> The Beggar to the Bush, then meet,
> And with Duke Humphrey (Heywood
> 1608, in Besant 1904:338).

Of course, ordinary townsmen and yeoman farmers could not
have afforded wine very often, the serf almost never so.
Taverns must have catered to those who could. The taverns of
London concentrated in commercial districts and around
permanent markets, those of other towns and cities around
markets. They probably drew a very mixed group of patrons on
market days, when both money and time were more widely
available, but a wealthier clientele at other times.

Country alehouses seem always to have attracted squires and minor gentry, yet in London the social segregation by neighborhoods would have mitigated against the like. In sum, no strict rules allocated social classes to drinking houses, but in practice the social rank of clientele varied _de facto_.

Evidently most taverns had as regular a clientele as the alehouses, but their typical town center locations must have attracted a much higher proportion of occasional visitors and strangers. The newcomer ordinarily found no obstacle; travelers remarked on the hospitality. Many premises were larger, more comfortably furnished, and more elaborately decorated than those of the alehouses, though contemporary descriptions may well have favored the more impressive establishments. Commonly there were several serving rooms, often, in later centuries, with waiter service, and meals were more the rule than the exception. Tables were often large, to accomodate large groups wining and dining together.

Coffee houses sprang up in Tudor London, followed the taverns in form, function and clientele, and by the eighteenth century rivaled the latter in popularity, the most so in London, but also in other cities. An eighteenth century design innovation of lasting importance was the provision of ample bar counters in both taverns and coffee houses (Gorham and Dunnett 1950:63-66). Taverns and coffee houses became even more than their predecessors places for the transaction of business or just haunts for tradesmen.

Stories circulated that most shopkeepers spent their days in this way and left their shops to apprentices (Besant 1902:298-301). But while taverns in the center of London tended to be quiet places for bourgeoise socializing, others were more raucous, hosting bull baiting and cock fighting.

From a wealth of contemporary description of eighteenth century taverns and coffee houses it is clear that men predominated at taverns and coffee houses, though women went to both. As for design, one can see hints of later public house layouts: one large, open room with bar counter, and smaller rooms offering more private settings.

The eighteenth century also witnessed the rise and fall of the London gin shops, which for a time drew the bulk of the trade away from the alehouses. From roughly 1720 until the raising of the excise on spirits (Act of 1753) occurred what become known as the gin epidemic. Hogarth's famous print Gin Lane attests to the widespread panic about the size of the trade, and mortality statistics bear out the contemporary opinion that alcoholism was rampant (George 1964:22). Once taxes went up the epidemic subsided and people returned to beer, but the whole episode would later be fully exploited by temperance advocates.

Conversation and drinking were the main fare of both taverns and alehouses, but games were also prominent activities. Finn (1966) describes the history of games. Backgammon was the medieval standby, while cards became fashionable in London taverns in the seventeenth century and spread from there. Shortly after, a variety of floor games, e.g., skittles, came in. Shuffleboard had been popular since the Middle Ages (Whitbread Library 1947:20). Many of the games played in modern pubs have a long history, although of the two current favorites, darts is recent and dominos formerly of far less importance.

Inns

During the twelfth and thirteenth centuries religious orders ended their practice of maintaining hospices, and inns took over the sheltering of travelers. Most were established at crossroads and in country towns. The cities held similar establishments, but few besides what rich burghers maintained for the occasional wealthy guest. In succeeding centuries commerce greatly increased, and English inns proliferated and become foremost among all travelers' accommodations in Europe.

In principle the inns sheltered all social classes, as at the Taberd of the Canterbury Tales, where knight, cleric and miller sojourned together. Yet too much should not be made of what society permitted. Villagers lived in a confined world, their horizons not extending far beyond the next village. The rural masses were tied to the land by poverty, villeins by law. For these people the inn would have had little import. Even for the poorer townsmen travel must have

been a rare event. It can therefore be assumed that higher
grades of society, in particular those inclined by profession
to travel, comprised the better part of the usual guests.

The inns had private rooms, usually upstairs, for those
who could afford them, and cheaper sleeping space in a common
or the kitchen downstairs. The care given the guest in a
private room was often impressive: stabling his horse, and
serving food and drink in his quarters (Moryson, In Rye,
1967: 272-273, Harrison 1968). There was thus at least a
symbolic social separation, even though guests frequently
availed themselves of the often lively society downstairs.

Trade Regulation and the Impact of Technical Innovations

Medieval manors and boroughs employed ale tasters and ale
conners to test the quality of beer brewed within their
jurisdiction. Ale conners wore leather breeches and would
sit in a pool poured on a bench, quaff a few pints, and
stand. If they stuck the ale was of poor quality; we would
now say it had too many unfermented solids.

The licensing of persons to sell beer dates from the
reign of Edward VI. The history of regulation is long and
complex. What is relevant here are those laws which affected
the vitality of the trade and the number and form of the
houses (Askwith 1928; Janes 1963; Monckton 1966; Pratt 1907;
Webb and Webb 1963).

As early as 1604 the Privy Councel laid down a policy, in terms that would echo down to the present, that alehouses "ought to be no more than a number competent for the receipt of travellers, and for the supply of wants to poor people not able to provide for any quantity of victual for themselves" (Webb and Webb 1963:8). The council also stipulated Sunday closing for all but travelers, a measure that would also often reappear. Licensing policy thereafter moved in cycles between suppression and tolerance, the overall trend being toward a reduction in the number of licenses (Appendix One).

Reduction raised the value of licensed properties and coincided with the growth of large breweries. Hops were in general use by the eighteenth century, their preservative effect enabling beer to be transported further. This, along with advances in mechanization, contributed to economies of scale, and large firms came to dominate production in urban areas. Whitbread led in London, brewing 63,408 barrels in 1690 and 150,280 in 1786. By 1791 nine breweries controlled almost half the London trade (Askwith 1928:14). The suppression of the gin trade may well have contributed to growth, but consolidation was inevitable in the emerging industrial nation.

Operations were hightly profitable, and a flow of capital reached the taverns and alehouses. The rising value of licences favored the buying of premises by brewers, laying the foundation of the "tied house" system under which tenants

lease from the brewer owner and agree to sell only, or
mostly, the owner's beverages. By 1818 one half of London's
pubs were owned and operated in this way (McGill 1969:8,
Matthias 1959:133). Outside of London the system evolved
more slowly, since aside from the makers of the famed strong
ales of Burton-on-Trent, the breweries grew more slowly.
Wherever tied houses developed, an important consequence was
that improvement capital and emerging concepts of business
management were brought to bear on them.

THE EMERGENCE OF THE PUB: 1830 TO WORLD WAR I

Eighteen-thirty is a landmark year, because in that year
Parliament passed the Beerhouse Act, both a response to
changes in the trade that had already taken place and
subsequently a major factor in the evolution of the public
house. By this time half a century of the Industrial
Revolution had passed, and the sweeping demographic, social
and economic effects of the epoch had reached the pubs. New
ideas of morality would soon leave their mark; the temperance
movement formed during the 1830's.

The terms "public house" and "pub" were in use by at
least the 1700's, applied to both alehouses and taverns, but
have been here reserved until this point for a reason. Their
use was universal after 1830, as the public house acquired
the variety of social functions and physical forms it would
carry into the present century. From this time on, "pub"

denotes an institution with its own special character.
"Tavern" fell rapidly out of use during this period, while
"beer house" continued to have some limited currency.

"Pub" then provides the starting point for discussions of
more recent change. This period sees the crystallization of
what will later be referred to as the "traditional" public
house, in its physical form and social function.

The Industrial Nation

Industrialization had several direct effects on the
market for alcoholic beverages. Because of urbanization the
majority of pubs were in the city, in crowded neighborhoods
with many potential customers close at hand. Industrial
wages increased the buying power of the masses. These two
factors favored the growth of larger houses catering to a
working class trade, but it was the changing structure of
society, the development of the class system of Victorian
England, that had the most profound effect upon the role of
the pub.

The explosive growth of the middle classes and the new,
industrial rich is well documented; England provides the
prototype of the nineteenth century bourgeoisie. The
increasing segregation of the classes was expressed not only
in patterns of residence and living standards but also in the
development of wholly different cultures, Disraeli's "two
Englands."

The working class was an uprooted lot. True, even the
poverty of which Dickens wrote was a relief from those
landless agricultural workers displaced by the Enclosure
Acts. Trevelyan (1954) argues that the lot of the London
laboring classes improved markedly from the eighteenth to the
nineteenth centuries, and testimony is ample that factory
workers enjoyed better living conditions than cottage
workers. Still, the development of the new neighborhoods
around the factories created vast areas of unrelieved squalor
on a scale not previously known. The growth of neighborhoods
based on little more than common means of employment meant a
loss of the close community life that many had left.

Unfortunately, not much is known about changes in the
organization and general life of working class families
during this time. Most of what is recorded is about the
stresses on families: apprenticing of children, long hours of
work, occupational diseases, and economic hardship.

Contemporary reformers observed that drinking increased
during the first half of the century. Many saw this as a
social disorder arising from the deterioration of home
conditions, and felt that alcoholism was rampant, on the
order of the gin epidemic. Per capita drinking did reach a
peak at mid-century, the time when the new wards of the
Industrial Revolution had deteriorated to their worst state
ever and Mayhew "discovered" the London poor, yet the figures
for consumption, while high, do not support the thesis that

alcoholism was universal among working men. Rather, it would seem that the homes were socially unfulfilling as well as decrepit, and this caused the pubs to have a greater role than would otherwise have been the case. This implies a lot of drinking and a lot of drunks, but not mass degradation.

The new middle classes became politicallly dominant after the Reform Bill of 1832, reflecting the influence they already wielded in society. Divorced from the working classes and alternately aping and rejecting the culture of the aristocracy, they molded what is thought of as the Victorian life style. The new society's cornerstones were the work ethic and stringent role separation of men and women. Evangelical Anglicanism and Nonconformist fundamentalism were the religions. From these sources stemmed an emphasis on respectability, the Victorian morality. Eventually the highest orders of society, not the least Queen Victoria, subscribed to the same concepts of respectability, all except some unruly country gentry.

Many pursuits now labelled immoral, or at least disreputable, had to be forgotten or practiced covertly by members of the middle and upper classes. Mistresses either disappeared or became less obvious. Drinking in public lost respectability. Even at home, a change took place:

> In 1830 and on into the forties men drank deep after dinner. If a gentleman was not in a fit state to join the ladies, his servant loosened his neckcloth and if necessary put him to bed, or if he were a dinner guest get him into his carriage and when arrived at home into his bed, and wives were so well used to this routine

that they accepted it as a matter of course. Queen
Victoria, however, aimed a blow at heavy after-dinner
drinking when she required her gentlemen to join her in
the drawing-room shortly after the ladies left the
dining-room (Peel 1934:117).

The quote describes the urban upper classes, but a turn
away from heavy imbibing at home was already evident in the
middle classes, especially those with Nonconformist religious
affiliations. Needless to say, drinking in pubs acquired
even more disreputability. Although relevant statistics are
lacking, all accounts indicate that non-working class
attendance fell off sharply, even though some "respectable"
men kept up surreptitious visits to the pubs.

The Temperance Movement

A consequencce of the middle class's estrangement from
the pub scene was their progression from viewing with
detachment to viewing with horror. Comprehension went
somewhere along the way. There was something very convenient
about drinking. It was manifest in working class
neighborhoods, and so was poverty, an association whose
explanatory potential was not long missed. To fatalistic
rationales of poverty offered by the gloomier economists was
added the notion that its worst manifestations were due to
demon alcohol. As late as 1902 the sociologist B. Seebohm
Rowntree, in a study of York, ascribed two thirds of the
poverty there to "secondary causes;" family income met a
minimum standard of subsistence (set by the author), but the

means were spent elsewhere. Drink was listed as the main
cause of "secondary poverty" (Rowntree 1902). Several
generations of parliamentarians pronounced that higher pay
for working men would simply be squandered on alcohol.

"Improvement" of the working class became the major
motivation of the temperance movement, which congealed after
1830. During the first two decades of the movement crusaders
who were not themselves abstainers commonly went out seeking
pledges of abstinence from the working class, a hypocrisy
that later largely ended (Gourley 1906). Radical reformers
formed the bulk of the early organizers, and continued to be
the major innovators and leaders for some time. In
Parliament the Liberal party and its leader of several
decades, Henry Gladstone, became associated with moves for
temperance legislation.

The other principal motivation for the movement was the
equation of drinking with sin, and as the century wore on the
spirit of a religious crusade developed. The concept that
drinking in itself is immoral was actually quite novel.
Heavy drinking had long been seen as just another excess,
much like overeating. Earlier commentators condemned
Glutton, of _Piers_ _Plowman_, for nothing more than gluttony,
though he drank a great deal, and denounced houses of drink
as loci of bad conduct, but because of activities secondary
to drinking. Suppression of houses was generally due to some
such suspicion on the part of the authorities. While some

reaction to spirits dates from the time of the gin epidemic, beer was always considered the legitimate and wholesome national beverage.

Carter (1933) traces three distinct historical phases in the temperance movement, differing in the strategies of the reformers. They are in chronological order the eras of "moral suasion," "legislative suppression," and decline.

During the era of "moral suasion," a concentrated propaganda effort was aimed at getting people, especially in the working class, to "take the pledge" and become abstainers. The period can be dated from the formation of the English Total Abstinence League, in 1832, which grew rapidly during the remainder of the decade, departing from earlier organizations in its rejection of beer as well as spirits. The Beerhouse Act of 1830 had removed all restrictions on the establishment of new premises licensed to sell beer. The object was to suppress a renewed growth of gin houses, but the proliferation of beer licenses caused a reaction which contributed directly to the formation of the League.

Pledges were circulated, the most in Nonconformist chapels, and a high proportion were returned by the upper strata of the working class, e.g., engineers and mechanics, many of whom were already committed to sobriety. Most of the hard drinking poor remained unconverted, and total consumption actually rose steadily.

Frustrated by their lack of success and encouraged by the experiment of the state of Maine in total prohibition, the movement moved into the phase of legislative suppression. A new organization was formed, the United Kingdom Alliance, which organized a political campaign directed toward the eventual goal of total prohibition. The greatest success was the Beerhouse Act of 1857, which repealed that of 1832 and restored the discretionary powers of the licensing justices. Later bills intended to move further toward the goal all failed, and in 1895 the Veto Bill, which would have greatly broadened the control of local authorities over the trade, was defeated in Parliament. The event marked the loss of Liberal support and the beginning of the decline.

The movement's greatest legacy proved to be the placement of a large number of temperance, even teetotal, minded men in the licensing justices' positions (Webb and Webb 1902). The effect was lasting and is evident in some places to this day. Reduction of the number of licences was accelerated, most notably in Liverpool, where a succession of temperance justices made the ratio of licensed premises to population the lowest of any major English city. At the end of the century many justices began to insist that pubs in their jurisdiction provide alternative activities, even alternative beverages, to those already supplied. Possibly these actions planted the seeds of the "improved public house" movement of the twentieth century.

The Workingmen's Club Movement

Also in the mid-1800's the workingmen's club movement began, clubs that would eventually rival the pubs as places for drinking, casual conversation and gaming (B.T. Hall 1922). The movement ironically began as an offshoot of the temperance movement, whose reformers established the first clubs, beginning, arguably, with one founded by Viscount Ingestre in 1852 (Whitbread Library 1950). Soon thereafter clubs were formed all over the country, many through the efforts of a Unitarian reformer, the Reverend Henry Solly. He and others formed the Workingmen's Club and Institute Union in 1862, which to this date enrolls most of the workingmen's clubs in England.

The early clubs had clauses in their charters banning alcohol, and much of their fare consisted of temperance lectures and courses in intellectual self improvement. This the clubs borrowed from the mechanics' institutes which somewhat predated them. Like the institutes and the pledge campaigns, mostly the upper sectors of the working class were reached, particularlly those individuals already heavily committed to the ethic of work, religion and sobriety. Membership lagged. Then in 1865 came a change:

> For twenty years the workmen tolerated it (the ban on alcohol). Lord Brougham was followed as president by Lord Rosebery, and then Dean Stanley of Westminster. 'Lady Augusta Stanley and the Dean frequently invited large parties to Westminster Abbey and to tea at the

Deanery.' Then, seeing no reason the normal process of
democratic election, which prevailed in the individual
clubs shouldn't apply to the central council too, they
pushed the proposal at the annual meeting. They even
proposed Bradlaugh as a Vice-President. The Dukes and
Earls all left. There were no more teas at the
Deanery. The working class took over the movement. It
only remained for them to bring their beer in, and
despite the assumptions of the industrialists,
aristocracy, clerics, and liberal reformers - there was
the germ for a movement which has given its shape to
working-class community. Said the first working-class
President, "Each club should be altogether free from
all vexatious infantile restrictions on the consumption
of intoxicating beverages and all similar matters"
(Jackson 1968:40).

The ban was relaxed everywhere in a trice, and in a few

years fell out completely. At the same time games began to

replace arid lectures. From this time on the clubs typically

offered a greater variety of games, entertainments, and other

recreation than did the pubs. Membership boomed. The close

tie between beer and workingmen's conviviality was

reaffirmed. Before 1900 the clubs were strongest in London's

East End, but thereafter grew most rapidly in the industrial

North and Northeast.

Development of the Pubs

The increased sales of spirits during the 1820's were not

in a plethora of dingy shops, in repetition of the gin

epidemic, but in new gin houses apparently constructed along

lines similar to the other licensed houses of the time. A

bar counter was a feature of at least one room, and other

rooms were used for drinking as well.

The Beerhouse Act of 1830 had unanticipated effects upon the trade, making spirits an especially lucrative, high profit margin item, and freeing capital for improvements in those retail houses. The competition of the growing number of beer licenses was met by creating elaborate premises to draw customers. Luxurious surroundings were not new - taverns and coffee houses of earlier centuries occasionally had almost fantasy trappings - but it was mainly in these "gin palaces", as they were termed, that the "frankly theatrical" line emerged as a continuing tradition (Gorham and Dunnett 1950; Janes 1963; Vaizey 1960).

The breweries and possibly some of the wealthiest independent publicans countered by creating some of their own "palaces." Later in the century most "palaces," whatever their origin, acquired licenses for beer, wine and spirits, and the separate designation of "gin palace" faded out completely. The "frankly theatrical" line continued. In addition most pubs in city centers and main streets radiating from the centers grew larger and more elaborate, if not quite to "palace" standards. After the 1857 Act "home from home," the descendant of the old alehouse, gradually retreated to the smaller towns and to back streets. The process was never completed; one room pubs can still be found almost anywhere. Small pubs especially survive in the South of England. Still, the large urban pub came to dominate wherever there was a sufficient concentration of potential customers.

One theme dominated the floor plan of most urban pubs: a "public bar," usually fairly large, supplied with a long bar counter, and a varying number of other rooms, generally smaller, which served diverse social functions. The need to provide service to all rooms was solved mainly by two methods.

The larger houses of earlier centuries provided waiter service from the storage area. The pub pattern that evolved gave waiters access to the rear of the bar counter in the public bar. Usually a hall at the rear of the public bar led to the smaller serving rooms, a plan shown schematically in Figure I.A.

The other solution was to provide direct service to all rooms by extending the bar counter. The surrounding space was partitioned (Figure I.B).

Of this central service plan Gorham and Dunnett wrote:

> The Victorian pub was a landmark in the evolution of pub design, for, in contrast with the earlier practice of linking, as required, a series of small rooms to a central service area by knocking down partition walls and opening up doorways, the customers' space and the service area were for the first time regarded as one unit, which then could be subdivided to fit the local needs (1950:74).

This statement describes well the functional differencce between the two plans. The central service plan never supplanted hall plans. The examples of pubs I have seen that have survived from the period mostly fall into the hall plan category. Apparently, Gorham and Dunnett were writing about

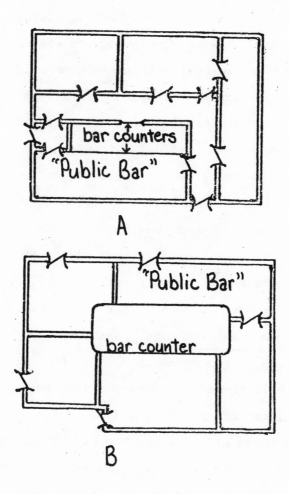

Figure 1.   Two Ways to Provide Service

pubs representative of the frankly theatrical tradition.
They do mention that the "Victorian" pub developed from the
gin palaces (1950:72). Surviving houses on this Victorian
central service plan are mostly found in commercial districts
of large cities, particularly in London, while the more
prevalent hall schemes dominated pub design in the North.

A number of rooms in a typical nineteenth century pub
retained the cozy features of the alehouse; often they would
be centered on a hearth. Others, very large or with ornate
settings, must have lost that feeling.

The more pretentious rooms acquired titles to match:
"wine bar," "saloon bar," "private bar," etc. (In Britain a
serving room is a "bar," a counter for serving drinks a "bar
counter"). In many, perhaps most, cases, the new room names
appealed to snobbery, the rooms themselves to people who did
not work with their hands. Naturally it was necessary to
take respectability into account, and provisions were made
with the two purposes of affording the middle and upper class
drinkers' some anonymity and insulating them from the working
men. Where there was central service, "snob screens" of
frosted and decorated glass were placed strategically upon
the bar counter. The "gentlemen's" rooms were either
provided with a separate exit to the street or the door to
the hall that lay nearest the street. In either case, access
was usually to a side or back street.

Furniture and decor followed the same pattern of social stratification as the rooms, and the prices charged for drinks also differed, sometimes on a distinct scale for each room. The higher prices partly covered the greater cost of furnishings, but the practice added to the effect of surrounding patrons with symbols of class distinction.

Furniture was nearly always threadbare in the public bar, fueling complaints that pubs had little purpose except to sell drinks. A customer with an emptied glass was left the alternatives of leaving, getting a refill, or standing around in a noisy, crowded room, a practice that Gorham and Dunnett (1950:72-75) particularly associate with the "frankly theatrical" pubs. Given that these represented a considerable capital investment, this would seem a logical strategy. Furniture in other rooms was progressively more comfortable the higher the prices charged.

Ornamentation reached a climax in all pubs of this period, a reflection of the tastes of the time. A distinctive style evolved, marked by certain styles of embossed metalwork ceilings, carved woodwork and frosted glass, all of which became art forms with their own corps of specialists. Ornamentation also varied with the social status of the room. The "snob screens" were often the most expensive single piece in the pub.

The little alehouses continued alongside the main urban traditions. The country alehouse became known as the country

pub, many added bar counters and decor and tended to imitate
on a more modest scale the styles of the city pubs. The
essentials of layout and social use remained unchanged. Much
the same can be said of the small urban pubs, whose survival
has already been noted.

"Hotels" replaced "inns." Their plush licensed rooms,
"wine bars," and later "cocktail bars" became fashionable,
designed to maximize an air of respectability. Eventually
"hotel" became a euphemism for pub, particularly in the North
where many "hotels" have never offered accommodation.

THE IMPROVED PUBLIC HOUSE MOVEMENT

An outgrowth of temperance sentiment was the so called
"improved public house" movement, which attracted
considerable attention between the two world wars. Operating
on the thesis that the traditional pub existed only to
promote insobriety, the movement's advocates proposed reform
of the houses as the way to combat mass drunkenness. Changes
of pub design, reform of sales practices, and the provision
of alternative activities were the main objectives.
Reduction of the total number of licenses was always part of
the plan. Management of the nonprofit Trust Houses,
established around England in the five years after 1908
provided precedents. However, the ideas gelled in the
improved public house movement and were carried out more
intensively and on a wider scale.

Frustration at the failure of legislative prohibition, in particular the defeat of the highly restrictive licensing bills of 1904 and 1908, resulted in much rethinking in temperance ranks. Pub reform groups appeared: the True Temperance Association in 1908, and shortly after the Fellowship of Freedom and the Scottish Public Houses Reform League. In 1909 the bishops (Anglican) of Worcester and of Chester made statements for pub reform (E.E. Williams 1924:12). These efforts resulted in a handful of "model" pubs but little more.

Though some inspiration came from the nonprofit Trust Houses, founded in the period 1908-1914, the real impetus for the movement came from the Carlisle experiment in state management of public houses (Carter 1918), from 1915 until dismantled by the Thatcher government. Carlisle housed vital munitions industries during the first world war and also had a notorious record for drunkenness. As a war measure the government took over the pubs of Carlisle and of nearby New Gretna and Cromarty Firth, Scotland, along with the local breweries that supplied them. Some of the Carlisle measures were never enacted elsewhere, i.e., managers with no vested interest in selling drinks and strict policing during the first few years, but the Carlisle pubs inpired other efforts in the 1920's as brewery agents and other influential parties went there to observe.

> Carlisle has in fact become a Mecca for a constant
> stream of brewers and their architects, as well as for
> licensing magistrates, temperance reformers and other
> interested persons (Oliver 1934).

The effect of the movement was uneven across the country, in the main because of variable enthusiasm among the brewers and differing policies of the licensing justices who had the power, under an act of 1902, to refuse any structural alterations in public houses. The Mitchell's Brewery and the justices of Birmingham made a deal by which several licenses, usually small houses near the city center, would be traded for a single license on the outskirts. The new licenses were earmarked for pubs on the "improved" model. The London Council promoted a limited number of "improved" houses in the vast housing estates it constructed during the 1920's and 1930's. Elsewhere scattered pubs were built along the same lines, notably in the cities of the Midlands. Resistance was met from the teetotal justices of Liverpool and a few other places. At a time when the existing rural pubs were in financial trouble, the movement remained urban.

The main sources on movement principles and pub designs are Gorham and Dunnett (1950), Vaizey (1960), E.E. Williams (1924), and Oliver (1934, 1947). As exemplified in Carlisle, Birmingham, and the outer London estates, there were four tenets of design.

(1) Provision should be made for extensive recreational activities oriented toward all adult members of the family, often for what were termed community-wide activities.

(2) An attractive and wholesome setting should exist throughout the establishment.

(3) Group meetings and "cultural" activities should be provided for in the facilities and actively encouraged.

(4) Management should promote alternatives to alcoholic consumption, in the form of soft drinks and meals. Food displays and cooking space, even separate kitchen space, should be provided.

These requirements obviously necessitate very ample facilities, and during the interwar years some truly enormous houses were built. This was especially true on the London Council estates, where the ratio of people to pubs ran as high as 10,000 to one. The average "improved" Birmingham pub was not a great deal smaller. A sample plan is shown on the following page in Figure 2. The rooms themselves were all of a relatively large size, ranging up to true auditoriums. At Carlisle,

> ...one of the first steps was the abolition of 'snugs' or 'snuggeries' -small drinking compartments almost impossible to supervise, but at that time a characteristic feature of public houses in the North" (Oliver 1947:58).

Central service was a nearly universal feature. Usually all the rooms had some length of bar counter, and wherever possible the service areas behind the counters were made contiguous. The purpose was to permit visual surveillance and easy management of all space. The rooms themselves spread away from the bar counters with seating space for

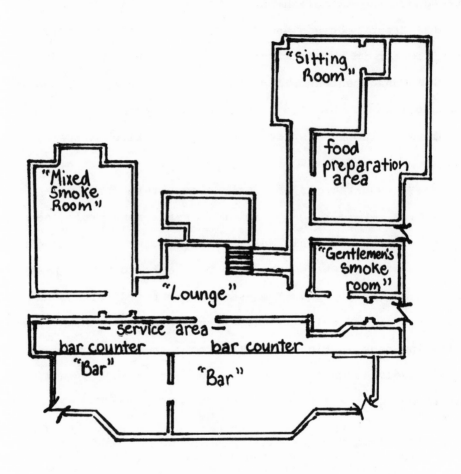

Figure 2. A Large "Improved Public House"

twenty or thirty, up to several hundred, people around tables
and on comfortably upholstered seats.

Surroundings were made "wholesome" by leaving open space
in the rooms, building in bright lighting and a number of
windows, using cheerful colors and small decorative touches
such as potted flowers and paintings of country scenes,
adding lanscaping outside, and in general dressing the
reformers' concepts of healthy surroundings with a dose of
working class sitting room features. Types of rooms new to
pubs appeared: auditoriums, rooms with diverse amusements and
games, and, above all, dining rooms.

Many ideas were carried to outlandish or impractical
extremes. The wide intervals between pubs in outer
Birmingham and the London County Council estates was
premature at a time when few of the intended patrons could
afford cars, and Vaizey (1960:122) suggests that clubs
flourished in these areas as a direct result. The
auditoriums never saw much use. I visited three of the
largest Birmingham houses built during these years, and found
that their auditoriums had been subdivided. These pubs now
have a multiplicity of rooms built on particular themes and
attract a young trade, hardly their originally intended
purpose.

Activities that were supposed to be culturally uplifting,
such as poetry and plays in the pubs, were very much a part
of the original plans but never got far beyond the

experimental stage. More usual working class entertainments
for large audiences, such as band concerts, remained chiefly
in the clubs.

The movement has nevertheless had a lasting effect.
Central service has become the rule today in most new pubs,
and is preferred by most licensing justices. Planners
widely accept some of the criteria of a "wholesome"
environment, lighting and interior decoration in particular,
and both soft drinks and the provision of food are picking up
momentum. Business considerations and official policy now
favor the consolidation of pubs into larger houses, although
the giants of the interwar period are not being duplicated.
All of these changes are due to a number of causes to be
discussed later, yet the precedence of the improved public
house is of great importance and may be seen in many of the
specific forms of recent pub change. The language of the
Morris Commission (1943) is markedly similar to that of
"improvement" advocates and represents a degree of trade and
government consensus at the time as well as a foretaste of
postwar policy. The movement thus leads naturally into a
discussion of pub design changes in the thirty years leading
to the time of this study.

PUB DESIGN

Basil Oliver (1947:58) tells about a Carlisle pub that was painted battleship gray, driving out the regulars until the room was repainted in warmer colors, when they returned. The incident is an extreme example of the effect the physical features of a pub can have on its clientele. Renovations, new decor, or added amenities are sometimes deliberately aimed to attract a certain custom. More commonly the pub and its habitues have grown up together, each molding the other through a gradual process of influence and selection. Whatever the case, the atmosphere of the pub is largely the result of the interaction of its physical environment and the people that inhabit it.

This chapter relates trends in design to pub culture. The focal point is the spatial relations within the pub: the uses of space, floor plans, specific settings and their social functions, and cultural determinants of spatial features. Decor and other stylistic features must be treated at least peripherally, since even general statements about the use of space must take them into consideration, but Chapter Five will deal more thoroughly with design features, how they are integrated with clientele and behavior into systems.

A patron not only has to select a pub, once there he must choose a space to occupy. Most pubs have more than one licensed room, and a large room can contain several distinct settings. A few predominant types of settings are traditional within pubs, types that reflect a consistent correlation between design and usage. To a degree, the names by which the rooms are generally called and the titles inscribed on the door coincides with the typology, but the titles tend to outlive their original meanings, and regional differences add to the confusion. Titles also do not reflect divisions within rooms.

Changes in pub design since World War II appear sweeping to most observers, an opinion which seems justified. Interestingly, no radically different settings have been created and few old ones lost, at least to date. Rather, the magnitude of the change stems from the increase of some settings at the expense of others, through renovations of floor plans and a selective policy of license reduction.

SETTINGS AND SOCIAL SPACE

Humphrey Osmond (in Sommer 1969) first distinguished "sociopetal" and "sociofugal" space, roughly that which encourages social interaction and that which does not. Traditionally the drinking places of the English speaking world differ in plan from the cafes and bistros of western Europe. In the latter tables form numerous sociopetal spaces, but these spaces are small, and the room as a whole presents an array of discrete social foci. In the British Isles the traditional plan favors more interaction within the whole room or within some major segment of it. Needless to say, Europe has its "homey" cafes, England its socially diffuse pubs, but the separate traditions are so often remarked upon as to seem a truism. The current vogue of "pubs anglaises" in France and other continental countries seems to be at least in part a recognition of the difference.

The English emphasis on sociopetal space is recognized in the vernacular. "Cozy" is a commonly encountered word, used in England generally with connotations of "home like" or "close." When applied to pubs, it coincides very well with "sociopetal," since in this context both would be applied to spaces which maximize interaction. Though pubs are often spoken of as cozy, specific rooms occasionally, tables are not.

Edward Hall (1959) calls attention to the wide variation among cultures in what constitutes social distance, i.e. the maximum distance of normal social interaction, the most that is comfortable to the persons involved. He remarks repeatedly how relatively great this distance is among North Americans. It is if anything wider among the English, at least in pubs, where I witnessed frequent interaction at distances of over twenty feet, with no apparent strain. Among North Americans twenty feet would be, in Hall's words,

"stretching the limits of distance" (1959:164), and in most
of the world would be unthinkably far. In practice the
determinants of social distance in a pub are very complex,
but the potential for maintaining socially satisfactory
interaction between all parts of a moderately large room
explains many of the unique features of design in English
pubs and should be remembered while considering the types of
pub settings.

THE REGULARS' CITADEL

Every pub has its "regulars," who nearly always have a
space of their own, at the least one they can take over
during peak evening and weekend hours. Most often pub design
is carried out with such a provision in mind. Whatever the
case, a type of setting results which I will call the
"regulars' citadel."

Not long ago the citadel commonly took up a whole room in
medium and large size pubs. The most widespread name for the
room was "taproom;" others include "snug," "newsroom,"
"parlour," "lounge," and a number of local favorites. In
small pubs, especially those without a prominent bar counter,
"public bar" was often applied.

The citadel is a consistent type because of its function
as a place where the male regulars spend long hours,
especially on evenings and weekend afternoons, talking and
gaming. They require a reasonably intimate environment and

modest comforts. As a result most regulars' rooms are models
of a sociopetal setting. They tend to be nearly square. A
number of tables, wall benches and chairs are provided, all
arranged around a central space, permitting easy conversation
with anyone in the room as well as creating a single social
focus. All this is "home from home," directly descended from
the old alehouse. Not long ago the hearth was nearly
everywhere a focus for the room. In large, urban center
pubs, central heating became general during the interwar
years, but elsewhere open fires remained the rule. Mass-
Observation (1970:93) gave one instance (in 1939) in which a
publican referred to a hearth in the taproom as "old-
fashioned, at that time more a harbinger than an accurate
reflection of trends. Figures 3.A and B illustrate two
contemporary but representative examples of regulars' rooms,
the first with a hearth and the second with none.

These plans illustrate the overall effect. Note
especially the central space. In observed rooms of this
type incoming patrons tend to fill the wall seats first,
turning their chairs to permit interaction with anyone in the
room. Although two or three separate interacting groups are
the rule during all but slack house, groups are repeatedly
brought together by exchanges of members and by extensions of
conversations, as in the following:

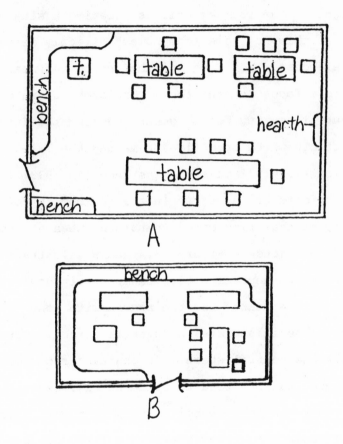

Figure 3.   Regulars' Rooms

at table) "Wasn't that a bloody awful go with

Blackpool? (across room) Did you see it, George?"

(across) "Is it you what hurt your back, Albert?"

(Field notes)

The dimensions of such rooms are well within the social

distance observed in all pub settings, since a wall twenty-

five feet or more is exceptional. Where a bar counter is

provided, it is short and does not intrude. Either the

landlord or a waiter provides service if there is no counter.

The resulting club-like atmosphere has often been noted.

It should be stressed that this is by tradition primarily a

man's world. Decor follows suit: dark colors, functional

furnishings, rough wood, linoleum or worn carpet, embossed

metal or plaster ceiling and walls, and everywhere the stains

and marks of heavy use.

THE CLASSIC PUBLIC BAR

"Public bar," "vault" in much of the North, denotes a

room in which the prices are at a minimum set by the brewer

or free landlord. In small houses, particularly in the rural

South and West, the "public bar" most often corresponds to

the description of the regulars' citadel, but more commonly

the term refers to a second type of social setting, which I

will name the "classic public bar."

Above all this is a place that working men can enter in

their dirtiest clothes and drink in while standing at the bar

counter, so the room is typically elongated with the counter
and a footrail running the length of the room, or angling to
the wall at one end. Furniture is sparse: a few rough
benches along the wall, two or three small tables, and
possibly a few wooden chairs. Before World War II a pile of
sawdust would lie in the center of the room, for spitting.

The predominance of workingmen in the clientele is
evident in the furnishings and decor. If anything these are
even more functional and sombre than in the regulars'
citadels, as well as more threadbare.

Figures 4.A, B, and C show floor plans of representative
classic public bars, all contemporary but little renovated
since the early years of this century. The only major change
would be the presence of tables opposite the counter where
once there was sawdust. The sociofugal effect is evident.
Not only are the patrons strung out along the counter,
everything is oriented toward the extended focus represented
by the counter. Social distance is exceeded at the extremes;
some very long bars of this type exist, even extending the
length of a city block. In this setting the lone drinker and
the small, isolated group are the basic social units. Groups
interact, but less than in the regulars' rooms, and the
classic public bars are far more often crowded, in which case
each little group of people is lost in the general jam.

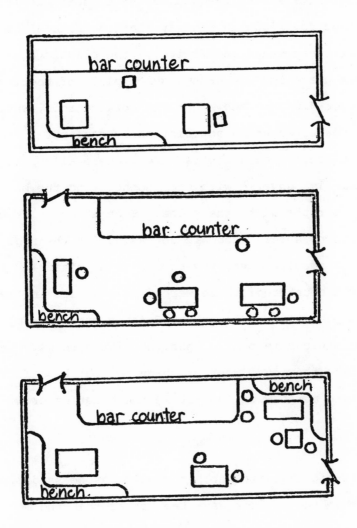

Figure 4.   Three Classic Public Bars

Regulars have always frequented the classic public bar, but it is not their own in the way that the citadel is. Drinkers will not stand indefinitely; the classic public bar is mostly a place for one or two quick pints of beer.

In Figure 4.C note the right side of the room, where there is created an uncharacteristically sociopetal effect. The seating focuses on a central area, where all patrons can sit and readily converse with one another, and the bar counter is peripheral to the scene. Such a layout is most common where no special room is set aside for the regulars, and seems to provide a variety of regulars' citadel. It is frequently encountered; there were five examples in the thirty-six pubs of the Bolton and Fenston primary samples. These spaces are more public than the little rooms. The regulars take them over most of the time, but have little choice but to merge with the mob in the event of crowding.

THE LADIES' ROOM

Not all regulars are men, though it may be said of women regulars that they have always been fewer than the men, and that they qualify with less frequent visits. In the small pubs women may be accommodated by being admitted to the regulars' citadel, but even in the country it is common for the landlady to invite them into her sitting room, which is usually licensed for the purpose. In the large houses a special room for women was prevalent before the second world war.

The title of "Ladies Room" went out of fashion early in this century, but is so apt it will be used here to designate the type. Since then, "Parlour" has been the most common title, but "Lounge" and even "Snug" are applied, along with the usual local variants and some inappropriate names left over from before renovations.

The floor plan closely follows that of the regulars' rooms, the dimensions if anything being smaller. The space belongs to the women, though men are allowed in and are on odd occasions the majority. The core of the patrons, those who maintain social continuity, is female and the trappings culturally defined as feminine: bright colors throughout, floral print wallpaper, upholstered furniture, potted plants and still life prints.

OTHER SMALL ROOM TYPES

Of other small, sociopetal rooms, the most common were formerly the "gentlemen's" rooms and those catering to young couples. Before 1939 rooms wholly dominated by the young were restricted mainly to very large pubs. They seem to have followed the ladies' rooms in floor plan and decor, but it is difficult to say much more about them. Older informants recalled little, while provisions for youth have undergone such sweeping changes as to make inferences from the present

highly unreliable. Of titles, little can be said except that
"Lounge" was common.

"Gentlemen's Room," "Private Bar," or "Saloon Bar" were
some of the titles once encountered on doors leading into
domains excluding working class people. Admission was often
only by permission of the regular patrons, in effect setting
up a club. These rooms were located mostly in bonafide
hotels and in public houses in commercial districts. They
were small and of course somewhat plush, but since the type
has vanished, little can be said about the social activity.

"Jug and Bottle" originally designated rooms that
accomodated a take-out trade in beer. Today the term
survives in country districts of the South, but the function
and social meaning are not consistent. In East Anglia most
are small regulars' rooms, with bar counters, in back street
pubs.

Diverse, less specialized little rooms were once
commonplace; one Bolton establishment had thirteen licensed
rooms in the 1930's, most quite small. Some carried overflow
from the larger drinking rooms and were not, in spite of
their size, settings for close social interaction.

THE LOUNGE

By now it should be obvious that "Lounge" adorns the door
of a variety of rooms. The understanding of nearly all
informants was of a room with the most expensive furnishings

in the house, but this rule has many exceptions. I even
encountered one battered, torn old room inhabited by the
outer fringes of society, a number of pickpockets included.
Bloody fights were commonplace, but "Lounge" was its title.

A number of modifiers are used in titles, giving rise to
"Saloon Lounge," "Ladies Lounge," and many others. All the
same, "lounge" commonly refers to rooms exhibiting some
consistencies in social use and design, an understanding that
will be followed henceforth.

A lounge by this definition is a fairly large room,
enough so that maximum social distance is commonly greatly
exceeded. Furniture is arranged so as to create a number of
independent social foci. In most cases the table becomes the
basic setting for social interaction, in the manner of the
European bistro, although in pubs the tables are usually
spaced farther apart. Trade promotional literature often
applies such adjectives as "open" or "airy" to the lounge. A
bar counter is usually present, perhaps less frequently in
the North, but waiter service within the lounge is common
during peak hours in large pubs. At the counter people may
stand several deep or sit on the stools provided, but in
other parts of the room they stand only during the crush of
peak hours.

A variation on the open space pattern is to create small,
sociopetal settings by subdividing the lounge. This is
accomplished by building alcoves into the walls or by using

dividers within the room: low counters, tall plants, etc.
There may be several tables, even encircling sofas or
upholstered benches, thereby enlarging the size of the
intimate spaces.

In some places, mostly in small communities, informants
held that before the last world war lounges were intended for
a middle class trade. This may have been true of those in
some localities, but lounges have been included in most
working class residential area pubs since the urban pub first
appeared, and many have carried the title. Some titles once
had a more definite class connotation, particularly the hotel
"Cocktail Bars" and the "Saloon Lounges" of London, rooms
that typically followed the lounge plan, but even these terms
have lost that meaning. Lounges, often multiple lounges,
often dominate those pubs that cater to a predominantly
middle class clientele, but the provision of lounges is but
one of many factors that attract the trade.

THE WHOLE PUB: TRADITIONAL LAYOUTS

The floor plans of small houses are harder to classify
than those of large pubs. The small pub is ordinarily also
the landlord's home, and licensed rooms are commonly
interspersed with domestic rooms on the ground floor. The
only major requirements are for each drinking room to have
access to an outside entrance and to the toilet facilities.
A central hallway or common entrance for the different rooms

is not necessary. A very regular clientele does not
absolutely require a convenient entrance, which may in rare
instances be deliberately hidden in the rear so as not to
attract strangers.

These reservations aside, two of the most common small
pub arrangements are shown in Figure 5.A and B, both from
pubs in the field sample. Note the absence of a hall in
5.A; front and rear entrances both open off the principal
serving room. Other rooms are entered through the main room
instead of the hall.

The need to provide service to a number of different
rooms limits the floor plans of the larger pubs. The two
main solutions are the same as in the nineteenth century:
building all rooms around a central service area, or
extending a hall through the "best" room area, in which all
the rooms have prices higher than those of the public bar.
The typical "palace" layout has been followed in few pubs in
this century, though complex central service arrangements
were essential to the plans of "improved public houses".

In the main pre-World War II design made use of central
hallways extending in back of the public bar through the
"best" section. In Figure 6 are two examples of the hall
plan, which differ mainly in the location of the regular's
citadel ("Taproom" in each) and the placement of the
entrance.

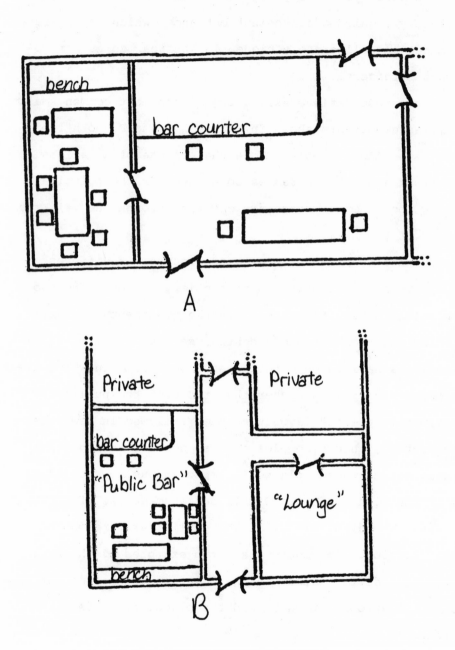

Figure 5.   Two Small Pubs

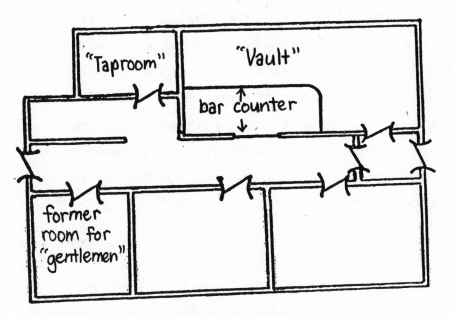

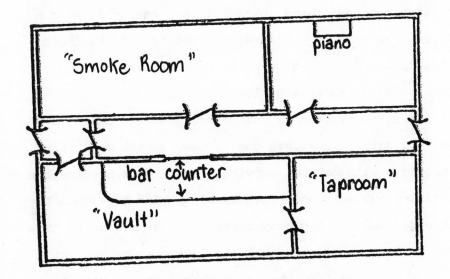

Figure 6.   Two Large Pubs

Each plan offers inconspicuous entry through the side entrance. The rear rooms off the hall are reached without encountering many people from the public bar or lounge. In Figure 6.A the rearmost room before World War II was a "gentlemen's" room, used mainly by local businessmen at the noon hour. Toilets presented a problem in pubs of this plan; they were rarely duplicated other than having both men's and women's. Absolutely rigorous social segregation would be unlikely in the absence of exceptional bladder control, presumably on the part of the "gentlemen."

POST-WORLD WAR II TRENDS

Officials froze public house construction and most alterations from the war's end until 1952, but the breweries had plans ready, and a subsequent boom in available money stimulated the most rapid changes in pub design in over a century. The pace slowed after the mid-1950's, but both construction and renovation continue today along the same lines as during the peak period.

The single, overriding change has been the consolidation of several small rooms into one or two, at the most three, all provided with central service. The lounge becomes the predominant pub setting. The classic public bar, though being edged out in some city centers, is otherwise in no danger of extinction, but the many little rooms are being rapidly eliminated from the large pubs. Their associated

social activities are transferred to the lounges and classic
public bars.

License attrition continues, the ratio of pubs to people
having dropped to 1:700 by 1969 (Appendix One). The axe has
overwhelmingly fallen on the smaller establishments. Added
to the pattern of renovations, the result is a drastic
reduction in the number of rooms that encompass a single,
sociopetal setting. New construction follows the same lines
as the renovations and results in the same overall plan.

While implementation varies greatly from brewer to brewer
and community to community, the brewers interviewed and those
who have taken a position in print agree that these trends
are necessary. The reasons are complex, but three are most
often cited.

(1) The licensing magistrates and other influential
public bodies tend to favor central service and large, open
rooms for the control they offer. The need to control
drunkenness and underage drinking is often cited, and the
justices are one source of local variation in the extent of
design change (Monopolies Commission 1968, Medlik 1969).

(2) As wages have risen and publicans' profit margins
have decreased, waiter service has become uneconomical
(National Board of Prices and Incomes 1969:15-20).

(3) Consumer demand favors the trends.

The last point is much debated. Brewery literature
represents the open lounges as modern, offering superior

service, and for these reasons a reflection of public demand.
Detractors may be found in any pub as well as in the press.
Their argument is that the breweries conspire to destroy the
old pub life in order to sell more drinks, and coerce and
brainwash the public to drink in mass watering troughs.
Interestingly both viewpoints may be found in the pages of
the Licensed Victuallers' trade journal, the Morning
Advertiser.

The argument is a variation on an old theme. Does
business create consumer demand or merely follow it? A
resolution to everyone's satisfaction is most unlikely, but
some suggestions will be made in Chapter Six when all the
factors governing the choice of pubs in a community are
considered.

Alteration is most often a merging of all the "best"
rooms into a single lounge. An extension of the bar counter
replaces a wall of the hallway. Figure 7 shows one typical
case, a Bolton pub before and after renovations carried out
in the mid-1950's, changes known from the testimony of old
time regulars and the evidence of old wall ends and other
features.

This basic alteration scheme has many variations. In the
North especially one finds a compromise between the older and
newer plans. The dividing walls on the "best" rooms side are
left in place, but the wall at the rear of the public bar is
replaced by a bar counter. Inside doors are removed and all

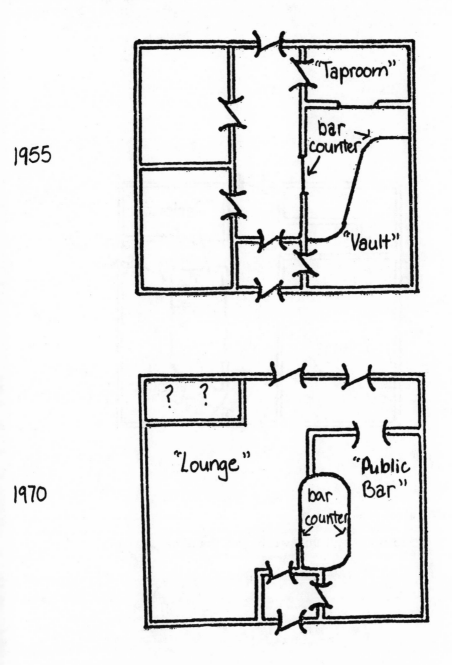

Figure 7. Alteration of a Bolton Pub

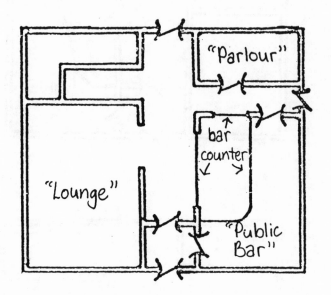

Figure 8.   Pub with Bar Counter in Hall

doorways widened.   An illustration is in Figure 8, again a

Bolton example.

The plan does not create a large, open lounge, but does

give customers in the "best" section access to the bar

counter, and the staff has fairly good control from behind

the counter. The main economic and judicial objections to

the old hall plan are therefore met. Nevertheless, this "bar

counter in hall" plan, as I would dub it, is not ordained to

survive in large numbers. New pubs, meaning mostly those on

new housing estates, are built on the large lounge plan.

Another variation is the complete elimination of the

public bar. A single lounge may be laid out on one or two

sides of the service area, or alternatively a vast area is

cleared or built surrounding the central service area,

divided only by walls with very wide doorways. Either way

the effect is more of a single vast lounge than of separate

rooms. One purpose of eliminating the public bar is to bring

all prices above the minimum. Many conjecture that the

public bar is doomed, that brewers and publicans are

conspiring to phase it out. Testimony before the National

Board of Prices and Incomes revealed the Licensed

Victuallers' officially stated wish to do away with the

public bar, but also significant grassroots support for its

continuation:

> Although there was some evidence of a diminution in the
> importance of the public bar in the two years reviewed,
> it was significant that over 20 percent of tenants
> attributed as much as 90 percent of their trade to that

bar. If free to do so, very few tenants - less than
ten percent (about 20 percent in London) - would close
their public bars entirely, although more would do so
during uneconomic trading hours. This finding is at
variance with the NFLV (National Federation of Licensed
Victuallers) submission and we are unable to agree with
their view that 'the public bar is a declining
institution whose demise should be accelerated'
(1969:17).

Most snugs and taprooms opening off public bars have been

eliminated. Whether the space is merged with the public bar

or made part of a lounge is often a matter of architectural

convenience. A snug placed near the entrance is absorbed by

the public bar. A taproom which is adjacent to the "best"

area likely becomes part of a central service area or lounge.

Small rooms and cozy settings are in no immediate danger

of disappearing altogether. The policies of breweries and of

local authorities allow for some small pubs to continue

indefinitely in both urban and rural areas. It is mainly in

these that sociopetal settings will survive, since

labyrinthine public houses are being steadily eliminated. In

the large houses public bars are now often shrunk to a

plausible size for a regulars' citadel, though they do not so

readily dominate the space as they once did a snug, or more

rarely a room is left for the same purpose on the "best"

side.

Though this type of space survives, growing numbers of

regular patrons see their local become a parking lot or its

inside walls torn away. They must travel further for a cozy

space, so defeating the traditional pupose of the local.

Must sociopetal space be lost? I would answer no.
Central service will predominate in all but the smallest
pubs, but this provision does not require opening up so much
space. Small rooms can surround the service area as in the
old gin palaces. Lounges can be subdivided, "bar counter in
hall" patterns used, or new design options developed; Gorham
and Dunnett put forth several innovative plans. And second
thoughts are indeed being entertained about the direction of
postwar design change. In Bolton most of the recently
altered pubs retain a small public bar, usually of a sort
that represents a compromise between the classic form, with
its casual use, and the regulars' citadel. Around the
country new or newly renovated lounges increasingly tend to
be subdivided, often with alcoves provided for darts and
other games. Possibly modern demands on the design of the
pub can be accommodated to traditional usage of the closer
settings, and something of the old alehouse kitchen can
survive after all.

THE PEOPLE IN THE PUB

This chapter sets forth a typology of pubgoers, a
fairly straightforward task but one that is subject to the
familiar qualification that the types do not take in
everyone. Many pubgoers and groups of pubgoers do not not
readily fit into any of these categories. Individuals may
at various times take part in different types of groups.
It is felt, though, that the typology is exhaustive at most
times in most pub settings.

THE LONE DRINKER

No social stigma attaches to drinking alone in public;
people are seen doing so in any pub. The lone drinker is
mostly left to his beer and his thoughts, and a number of
controls exist for assuring his privacy. Rarely her
privacy: I occasionally saw women drinking alone in pubs,
but not one who made a habit of doing so.

Regular lone drinkers are overwhelmingly beer drinkers.
In two nights each in Fenston and Bolton, notes were made
of the drinks of precisely fifty loners. Two drank
spirits, three sherry or port, and the remainder beer.

The Lone Stranger

Whether or not an unaccompanied stranger is brought into a group depends on a number of factors, notably one that is a little imponderable, the fit of his personality with those of the other drinkers present. In any event overt hostility or marked coolness towards strangers are very rare, a contrast with Cavan's (1966) experience in San Francisco, where newcomers were made to feel unwelcome in a considerable number of bars.

Custom in uncrowded or intimate surroundings is to give signs of recognition and reception to the stranger. These are pretty much the same as for anyone else: some form of hello on entering and "cheerio" or "ta ta" (North) when he leaves. The English do not accord such a greeting in most other public places. For the stranger the farewell is apt to be a bit louder and more unanimous than for the regular, but it would be wrong to infer that people are glad to see him or her go. In an uncrowded pub the overall attitude toward the stranger is friendliness, but friendliness expressed with more reserve than warmth.

The stranger typically stays only for the duration of a pint. A few may play with some amusement device or listen to the entertainment if any is available. Nevertheless, a man becomes a stranger when he finds himself out of his usual haunts and in a passive way desires the environment

of a pub, but just for the "pint." If he fancies more than
one pint, he very likely goes to more than one pub.

The stranger may be invited to join a group on his
first visit, especially if he stays on for more than one
drink, but this would be common only in areas exceptional
for their ready hospitality. Repeat visits arouse
curiousity, and the patrons begin to feel him out, asking
trivial questions about the weather and trying to find out
why he is in the area. From this point on, depending on
the fit of personalities and on a complex set of cues, the
stranger becomes either a member of a group or a regular
lone drinker.

The Regular Lone Drinker

Most who visit often and alone stay for only a pint or
two, there being only a few who spend the whole afternoon
or evening in one pub. They then go home or to another
pub. Quite a few go from pub to pub, on a regular round,
taking a drink at each. One Fenston man of about seventy
was so punctual that he arrived at each pub in turn at the
same time every evening.

The established loner is ordinarily past the age of
certain young, unmarried men who also drink alone a great
deal. While older loners are conceded their privacy, their
younger counterparts are often brought into bachelor
groups, which tend on the whole to be highly gregarious,

TABLE I

MARITAL STATUS OF REGULAR LONE DRINKERS

	Bolton		Fenston		England and Wales(1970) percent of male pop. over 34 that is single
	number	%	number	%	
single:	23	56	14	67	9
married:	12	39	5	24	83
widowed or : divorced	2	5	2	10	8

often to the point of absorbing all age mates who happen to be in the pub at any one time.

It was possible to determine the marital status of 62 men, 41 in Bolton and 21 in Fenston, all of them regular lone drinkers at pubs in the primary sample, and a disproportionate number were single. No women were encountered who habitually drank alone; the regular loner, as typified here, is male. A summary of the results appears in Table I, along with comparative percentages of men 35 and older in England and Wales in each marital status.

Obvious drunkenness is rare among the loners. This contrasts with the United States, where the lone drunkard is a fixture of most neighborhood taverns.

It is out of the compass of this report to dwell upon what motivates the lone drinker, but it can be readily seen that he derives social satisfaction in the pubs, however limited that might appear. Regular lone drinkers tend to be shy as well as single, awkward in a variety of social situations, not only in the pubs. On entering the pubs they are greeted warmly, perhaps more so than the other regulars. When the setting and crowd conditions permit, other patrons sporadically bring them into the more public conversations. The landlord and other staff are customarily cordial. Gentle joking relationships with both regulars and staff are quite common.

Assorted events involve the loners more intensely: darts matches and other contests, group sings, and other special occasions. Reactions vary, but the majority fit in easily and lose some of their normal reserve. When the normal social environment returns, they again detach themselves.

In pubs where traditional floor plans prevailed, observations found the loners more in the public bar than any other room. The "perpendicular drinking" arrangement favors the brief visitor. The classic public bar also best fits the social needs of the loner, giving him just enough anonymity without his being placed among strangers. However, loners are found in nearly every type of setting. The regulars' citadels have their share. As seats fill, there is the loner, sitting among people familiar to him yet retaining his status, taking occasional part yet not being fully integrated into the conversation and other activities.

One outcome of pub alterations is the displacement of lone drinkers into the lounges as the close settings are eliminated. Many stand near the lounge's bar counter, much as they would in the public bar. The area near the bar counter may reproduce the casual drinking and undemanding social environment of the public bar. Others sit at the tables, particularly under crowded conditions. The loner may find a place among the regulars if they have carved out

a citadel somewhere in the lounge, but more commonly the
lounge offers the loner a diminished social involvement.
It is apt to be too crowded, too open or too filled with
couples and other groups not readily accessible to him.
When sitting at a table under crowded condiitions, he is
not likely to have a first name relationship or other
familiarity with the people nearby.

Thoughts about the loner are private, since publicly
expressed opinions tend to be cliches. Ill words are not
spoken of him; he is a "good one" or "tops." It is hard to
say what emotions lie behind the deference, yet this
attitude is part of a whole set of behavior which
guarantees the loner's role in the traditional pub. It,
along with the greetings, the joking and the trivial signs
of recognition all accord him a place. Loners in the
lounge are more alienated from the social environment.
Some may prefer the greater privacy. Most have the option
of moving to the public bar or seeking out a more
traditional pub. Their motivations are less accessible
than the simple social fact of their growing isolation.

"MATES"

Most pubs would go broke without the "mates," in
popular usage a frequent assemblage of friends, ordinarily
men, in the pub context those men with whom one interacts
often and closely. Their base is their local, where they

form the core of the regulars. Some male groups frequent
many pubs without making one their local, but such habits
are surprisingly uncommon among working class patrons. In
a handful of pubs in the field study women were "mates,"
but in all cases they were young singles in pubs which
catered to that age bracket. It would be tempting to write
that they are "mates" because their role in the pub
corresponds to what is usually a male perogative. This may
well be true, but the relevant cases were too few to
support or refute the generalization.

"Mates" mostly fall into five classes. People in each
class tend to congregate together, but not usually to the
point of segregating themselves from other patrons, "mates"
or otherwise. The classes are (1) bachelors, (2) young
marrieds, (3) older marrieds, (4) widowers and old age
pensioners, and (5) workmates.

The latter are a special case, men who work together
and go to the pub in a group at the lunch hour or
immediately after work. Age segregation is exceptional.
In many cases they seem to work in the same section and
just naturally go off together for a beer. Most belong to
another group of "mates" at a local near their home.
Except in a small town workmates do not usually socialize
with one another at pubs away from work, and few of the
"mates" found together at pubs in the primary sample
evenings and weekends worked at the same place.

The bachelors are set apart by their lack of
conflicting ties to a wife and children and their differing
expectations of pub life. The old age pensioners and
widowers have in common their age as well as a lot of time
to spend. That the marrieds at most pubs divide by age is
not surprising, but for reasons that are not clear the
split in pub after pub was into two categories.

All of these groups engage in pretty much the same
activities. Conversation predominates, and all play the
usual pub games, and join in teams, social clubs within the
pubs, and other organized activities. On the whole the
bachelors take part in these less often than the other men,
but not enough so to make them any less a part of the
coterie of regulars. The bachelors tend to be regulars at
more than one pub and to wander to a greater extent than
the older men. More than anyone else they go on "pub
crawls," walking tours of pubs, drinking a pint at each,
until everyone is thoroughly drunk, but pub crawls are more
talked about than carried out; to my knowledge I happened
on only two in the course of the field work.

Except for the workmates, all of these groups tend to
meet at the pub. Sometimes a time is prearranged,
generally at the last time they were together, but more
often no firm plans are made, only an understanding of when
they will most likely be at the pub. This means in
practice that the group is together in its entirety mainly

on special occasions, e.g., darts matches. Some customary
times bring together most of the "mates." Sunday afternoon
is almost universal. An evening, often the one after
salaries are paid, is understood to be such a time in most
communities and is known as "boys' night," but the custom
is declining.

At other times members of the group wander in alone or
with a friend. If any of the "mates" turn up, they will
probably join together. Otherwise another group may be
joined. A regular who comes in alone may very well stay
and drink alone or talk with the staff. There are
different degrees of "mates" too. Those with whom a man
drinks most of the time are the ones he will probably join
if they are around but if not he will join other regulars.

Women

Some folk terms that classify women patrons are more
specific than the "mate" applied to so many different
males. These terms are applied to women individually and
in the company of men, but most persistently to those in
all female groups. "Old dears" and "birds" are more or less
stereotypic, and a large number of women, married ones in
particular, are not called by these or any other special
term.

The popular image of the "old dear," in the pub
context, is of a woman with graying hair, wrapped in bulky
woolens, sipping sweet stout with a bunch of women who look

just like her, gossipping and passing around pictures of
her grandchildren. A few fit the stereotype to a tee, but
not many, and the term is in practice applied much more
broadly. The most consistent characteristic of those so
called was that they were over forty. What became clear
during the fieldwork was that when the staff or the
regulars talk about "the old dears," speaking of those in a
particular pub, they are defining them in terms of the
women's role in the pub. The "old dears" enjoy a special
status within the house, not a little matriarchal, and
dominate a particular setting that is customarily their
own. They usually have husbands who are regulars at the
same pub. A "ladies' room" or space with similar function
is apt to be shared with younger women regulars and with
women their own age who are infrequent visitors as well as
with some of the men, but the "old dears" tend to dominate
the conversation there. It is for them that most
alterations in the space will be made.

     The term "old dear" is used in many different contexts
about which I do not know enough to say whether the pub use
is typical. A matronly connotation was suggested, however,
in the definition of one informant who offered, "An old
dear is somebody's mum."

     "Birds" is applied to any young unmarried women, more
specifically to any group of the same. It has no special
meaning in the context of the pub. "Dolly birds" is a

common variant. Their pubgoing habits are those of the
young in general; though the younger male "mates" tend to
wander a bit more, some groups of young women will go to
several, scattered pubs in an evening.

The remainder of the married women are set off here by
being neither single nor "old dears," though their
activities do not set them apart from the other women.
Conversation and listening to entertainment, where
available, comprise nearly all the activity. Women in
mixed groups play pub games a great deal, especially darts,
but not often in all female groups.

In spite of similar activities the habits of the three
types of groups set them apart from one another. The "old
dears" tend to pass a whole evening or Sunday afternoon at
the pub, although few go to the pub more often than once a
week. The remainder of older women who go to pubs are less
frequent visitors and may not even have a particular local.
They tend to be at the pub an hour or so, to get away from
home with a sister or just to accompany their husband to
the pub before he goes off to the public bar.

Mixed Groups

Lone couples form a sizeable part of pub clientele,
above all in the lounges. Young couples are more apt than
most patrons to sit off by themselves. They may
subsequently join other people, often by prearrangement,

but more than other patrons they can set themselves apart
and assure their privacy by sitting some distance from
anyone else. No bits of conversation are directed their
way nor other means used to bring them into the group.
Custom provides that their privacy is protected.

Groups of two or three couples, especially if young,
often sit off by themselves. They are then granted the
same privacy as the lone couple, and for the same reasons.
Young couples also enter into more gregarious mixed groups,
and a variety of cues signal whether they are to be left
alone or brought into social exchanges.

Many large, mixed groups of young people, often made up
of couples or a mix of couples and unpaired men and women,
act much the same as the bachelor "mates," and may even use
that term of address among themselves. In most communities
they inhabit the same settings as the bachelor "mates,"
participate in many of the same activities, and if cars are
available may be as migratory.

Other mixed groups tend to adapt to the setting in
which they find themselves. For example, a husband may
dress specially to join his wife in the ladies' room or
lounge and while there change his usual pub conversation
from sports to neighborhood topics. In like manner, where
a strongly masculine setting, i.e., a classic public bar or
regulars' citadel, is open to women, any female there is
apt to talk about football or play darts.

Swearing is normally suppressed in the company of women, but this rule does not always hold where women by their presence breach custom. In a betting shop in a Yorkshire mining town, a woman who invades that exclusively male domain risks having sexual comments directed at her. In the same town this also happened at least once in a normally all male pub (Dennis, Henriques and Slaughter 1956:213). In Newcastle-upon-Tyne, where women are not seen in many of the public bars, several informants stated that any woman who did enter had only herself to blame for what she heard.

MECHANISMS FOR MAINTAINING GROUP SOLIDARITY

Limits on Behavior

Various customary limits on behavior curb divisiveness within the group. For the most part pub behavior follows English cultural norms, but it also has its peculiarities, both special license and special curbs.

Most behavior that falls out of English cultural bounds is of course banned, but some behavior which is beyond the pale in most environments is permitted in some pub settings. Public obscenity among men is mainly restricted to all male environments at work or in some part of the pub. A more significant example would be the behavior associated with joking relationships. At the King Alfred,

Fenston, certain of the regulars joked about one another's
occupation, especially about that of one who is a dustman
(trashman). The comments would not have been considered
especially impertinent elsewhere, just out of place in
public. However, the degree to which personal jokes can be
made without offense is less than I have observed in North
American taverns, let alone in some of the cultures noted
for the development of joking relationships.

Aggression must never be implied within the group. It
is instead directed toward outsiders, mostly in mild verbal
form, and not even aimed directly at a particular person.
If about an individual, aggressiveness is usually expressed
in comments made to others within one's group, as when
someone pushed past a group to order at the bar counter;
"cheeky bugger" remarked a man to his friends. Someone
being edged out might say to the intruder, "here now" or
"easy." Such comments are made repeatedly in a crowded pub
in which the groups are not all on close terms. No offense
is taken as long as the remarks are not personal. On the
other hand, "cheeky bugger," if overheard, could start a
fight. Yet matters rarely escalate. Though the younger
men talk about pub fights, I only witnessed two. Despite
their mild impersonal nature, comments about those outside
one's group underline the "we-they" distinction, and the
rules of group interaction exaggerate the effect of design
and crowded conditions. In a sociopetal environment,

groups converse back and forth; the tendency is to draw in even strangers. In a sociofugal environment, conventional behavior reinforces the separateness.

Some conversational topics are off limits, particularly politics and religion, as well as anything that might be inflammatory in a given context. During the field work I never heard a conversation about religion in a pub. Six political discussions were heard in four different pubs, always when only the regulars were present and privacy assured. Publicans agreed that it is good policy to steer conversations away from these topics. In Bolton, where I heard only two political discussions, the Mass-Observation team found that eight percent of a sample of one hundred and fifty seven conversations were political in content (1970:187). The difference between their findings and mine probably stems from the fact that they were doing their field work during the great depression, a time of political ferment. In the late 1800's, a time of industrial strife and grass roots political organization, some pubs quartered organized political activity, including the formation and meeting of unions and cooperatives. Originally, "news rooms," which date from the period, were places in which journals and newspapers were stocked, at a time when mass distribution of news was considered subversive in many quarters. It would seem that in times of heightened political activity the rule of no politics in pubs is

eased, and perhaps people congregate according to their
particular stance.

Acts of Group Solidarity

Affirmations of group solidarity take verbal and
nonverbal forms. Some are simply a matter of reference, as
in the expression "me and me mates." Others are peculiar
to the pub environment.

One practice stands out sharply, "standing rounds," the
almost universal custom of taking turns buying drinks for
everyone in the group. Women are partly excepted. Men
tend to buy the drinks for a couple, but married and
unmarried women commonly reciprocate from time to time, and
a few insist on doing so most of the time. In most larger
groups women neither stand one of the early rounds nor buy
as many altogether, but they do buy some. Etiquette calls
for the women to at least offer to buy at some point,
though the men may keep the buying to themselves. A man
will buy drinks for a woman whose acquaintance he is trying
to make. Her acceptance is a necessary sign that she wants
to continue, and her offer to buy a round another favorable
sign.

Pressure is on the men to buy and to drink. An
exception is men who opt out of the custom altogether and
neither buy nor accept rounds. "I buy me own and no one

else's," as one Fenston man used to say. The stance is

accepted but is rather rare.

Invitations to join a group reflect the custom of

buying rounds, "What are you drinking, mate?' or "Charlie,

a brandy and Baby-Cham for this cockney bloke." The

practice has a long debated secondary function of promoting

drinking. Most overt drunkenness is seen among large

groups of drinkers exchanging rounds. Mass-Observation

(1970) concurs:

> Standing rounds is a form of social compulsion of
> great advantage to the brewers. It makes people
> drink more, and even spend what they can't
> afford...The effect of making people drink more than
> they mean or want is particularly noticeable among
> groups of young drinkers on Saturday nights (p. 179).

The authors go on to describe the competitive aspects

of the custom among young Bolton pubgoers, implying older

drinkers are not as competitive. On the basis of my own

observations, in Bolton and elsewhere, I would agree with

most of their statements, after adding that greater

affluence and a diversification of drinking habits have

changed matters a bit. Drinks are always equated on a one

to one basis, a severalfold variation in both price and

alcoholic content notwithstanding, and the effects on both

the pocketbook and the metabolism inevitably fall more

heavily on some persons than on others. Women can opt out

of the alcohol consumption by switching to soft drinks, but

men cannot ordinarily do so without losing face; the most

commonly accepted reason, having to drive, does not apply
to most men at any given time and is not always accepted
graciously.

The competitiveness of youthful drinkers is
demonstrated by their relatively hurried pace, compared to
older drinkers, and by their keeping an eye on one another
while all the while denying the effects of the alcohol on
themselves. Some brag about their capacity, but this is
considered poor manners even among neophytes. Older
drinkers try to act as sober as possible around others and
deny being drunk, but are not so anxious to show they can
outdrink the other fellow. The formal drinking bout is gone
along with the yard of ale and other accompaniments of past
centuries.

In recent years some customs closely related to
standing rounds have died out. All had the common
characteristic of demonstrating group solidarity through
reciprocity in drinking. As near as I could determine, the
only one which was still widespread in living memory was
that of "passing the glass," whereby persons in the group
would drink in turn from the same glass. The practice was
not reported by Mass-Observation, although Fenston
informants recalled it from the 1930's. Since that time,
"passing the glass" seems to have died out throughout
England.

Among verbal recognitions of the group the drinking of
healths stands out. This must be considered an expression
of good will, no matter how mechanically it is offered.

THE REGULARS

Regular, in any pub, is applied to people who are at
various times members of a number of different groups, yet
form an aggregate, a coterie that is the heart of the
traditional pub. One is considered a regular because of
the way one fits into the pub's society and not because of
any arbitrary frequency of visits. There is of course some
relation of the role with how often one visits the pub.
Nearly all male regulars come in at least once a week, most
of them two or three times, and certainly any person who
comes in daily is considered a regular, but some people
rarely visit and are still so classed. Informants, when
asked how often a person must come in to be thought of as a
regular, showed little agreement, and most often greeted
the question with bewilderment.

This usage of "regular" fits the social role of the
people included and corresponds to popular usage. It
implies a high degree of social integration within any
group known as "the regulars." The collection of regulars
at any pub includes one or more groups of "mates," some
loners and other people all tied together by common status
within the pub. I performed the experiment of asking

frequent visitors who they considered to be the regulars.
This was done with thoroughness, taking in nearly all
patrons on a busy evening, in four houses, a small one and
a large one in both Bolton and in Fenston. The purpose was
to determine whether the regulars are a well defined and
integrated group.

In the small pubs informants, including the staff,
agreed closely. The regulars would name one another, each
giving a fairly complete list.

Several overlapping networks appeared in the larger
pubs. Those of a Bolton pub are diagrammed in Figure Nine.
Each line connects two individuals, one or both of whom
named the other as a regular. Individuals generally named
most or all of the others in their own immediate circle and
a smaller percentage outside of this group. The pub
included a public bar and two lounges. Three of the four
subsets of regulars wandered among all rooms, although
there was a partiality to certain territories, and the
remaining group had staked out the rear of the public bar.
Both here and in the large house investigated in Fenston
the landlord named nearly everyone in the whole set of
regulars. The Fenston house included two lounges, each
with noticeable subdivisions, and each set of regulars had
its own territory fairly well marked out.

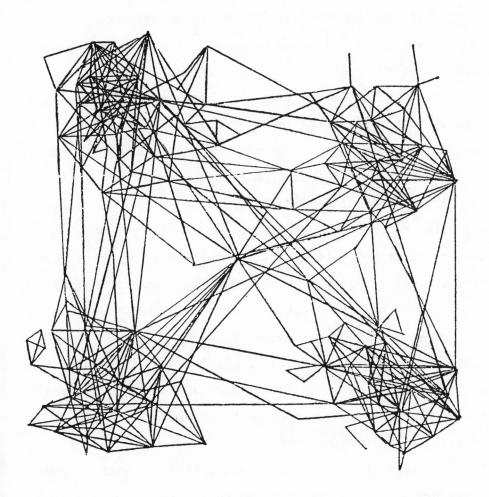

Figure 9.   Sets of Regulars in a Large Bolton Pub

In contrast, at some pubs with a very large trade of occasional customers, particularly certain Bolton, Newcastle and Bethnal Green pubs that offer entertainment, landlords named only a small group of men as regulars. This would indicate that where many people use a house as a local, the regulars tend to segment into subsets, but a small, tight set of regulars can maintain their identity even where greatly outnumbered by more casual customers.

Informants' definitions of "regular" tended to stress a belonging to one pub or the maintenance of a presence; a crucial point seems to be that, except at slack hours, some of the regulars are always around. The characters may change, but the play stays the same. The individual is part of the set because anytime he enters the pub, he is taken into one of the groups of regulars or, if a loner, is given the usual signs of recognition and brought into the system of social interaction noted before. It is significant that the circles of regulars illustrated in Figure 9 include some regular lone drinkers. Without their being members of any group of "mates," their status as regular was still awarded in such a way that they seemed to belong to one subset more than the others.

The regulars set the tone of pubs unless they are exceptionally few relative to the total clientele. If they are noisy and outward going, others follow suit. What struck me most about those large pubs that retained sets of regulars was how much they seemed to carry on as if they were in a back street, one room pub. They have their little territory wherever design permits, special recognition from the staff, and often the standard pub games to themselves. In some ways they inhabit a pub within a pub.

The total number of regulars in the smaller Fenston pubs ranged from twenty-eight to over fifty, probably typical of small houses. The circles of Figure 9 also fall within this range, suggesting what seems to be true generally, that sets of regulars segment before getting much above this range.

A variety of voluntary associations found within pubs symbolize membership in a particular house and offer inducements to come in and interact with other members. These are dominated by the regulars and help define that role. The most widely encountered and important are listed below.

(1) Social clubs are what the name implies. They are formed to sponsor occasional gatherings in the pubs, both formal meetings and parties, as well as special outings once or twice a year, such as picnics and excursions to the beach. They may also have the function of coordinating competition in games, both within the pub and against outside rivals.

(2) Teams compete against other pubs, clubs and whoever
else may sponsor a team. Most communities have leagues.
Competition is most commonly in darts, dominos and
sometimes cribbage, although bowls, skittles, pigeon racing
and many other games may have local importance.

(3) Mutual aid or risk sharing societies are varied,
but two types stand out on account of their nationwide
occurrence; "sick" or "slate" clubs, and "thrift" clubs.
"Sick" and "slate" clubs are sometimes distinguished by the
way they are organized, but not consistently, and the two
may be considered fundamentally the same. Everyone pays in
a regular amount, most often biweekly, and benefits are
paid on a set scale to sick members and to the widows of
members who die. Payments and benefits are today smaller
than in more customary insurance plans, but the principle
is the same, one of cooperative risk sharing. In the
"thrift" clubs money paid in regularly is drawn out just
before Christmas. The "sick" clubs pay out their excess at
about the same time. The pay ins are minor social
occasions, even though money is often brought in by proxy
or payment delayed several weeks. "Pay out night" is a
major event to which nearly all members go. A sizeable
amount of money is set aside from the funds for drinks, and
the publican supplies snacks. One meets members of these
clubs today who used to spend far more time in that
particular pub than they do today but still come in for the

"pay out night." Club membership and the accompanying
social occasions enable them to retain their status as a
regular, though they may now come in only rarely.

All of these associations have officers and usually a
written set of rules. In recent years some breweries have
started acting as treasurers for the clubs, insisting on
orderly bookkeeping, investing the money, and paying back
interest, which goes toward the party.

Although very few pubs' regulars and staff make
outsiders feel unwelcome, some favors are awarded the
regulars and no one else. During World War II, when beer
and other alcoholic beverages were rationed and often in
short supply, many pubs allowed more beer for their
regulars than for others, the relative amounts depending on
supply. Some Fenston pubs closed for everyone but the
regulars. A contemporary favor is that a pub stays open
after legal drinking hours, in most cases for the regulars
only. The occurrence of this practice depends a great deal
on the zeal of local officials. In general the smaller
pubs are more apt to stay open in this way. They are less
likely to be discovered, less likely to bother the police
if found out, the relationship between the landlord and the
regulars is apt to be close, and the landlord is more
likely to need the extra money to make up for his smaller
take during legal hours. A publican is everywhere expected
to remember the usual drinks of the regulars more than

other guests, to give them special greetings and in other
ways to recognize their status. This sort of recognition
is usual in even the largest pubs.

Certain facilities are often reserved for the regulars.
Cribbage and dominos equipment are kept stored. Outsiders
can request their use and challenge into existing games,
but playing is generally initiated and dominated by the
regulars. On the other hand, darts boards are available on
a first come, first serve basis. Regulars have no special
priority. The boards are readily available. Some crude
darts are ordinarily kept next to the board for anyone's
use, though the serious player uses a private set to which
he or she is accustomed. Many publicans keep the regulars'
own dart sets behind the bar counter.

Added together, these special recognitions of the
regulars accentuate the difference between one's own local
and the other pubs to which one goes. At the local one is
made to feel at home, hence the recurrence of "homey" when
informants describe their local or the ideal one.
Elsewhere one may have a good time but will be somewhat set
apart from those regulars.

THE STAFF

A discussion of the people who inhabit the pubs would
not be complete without touching upon the publican, the
publican's spouse and the hired staff.

"Mine jovial host," a beaming, beefy, beery Falstaff, as much one of the cronies in front of the bar counter as a salesman behind it, is the publican of lore. In the little houses the ancient tradition of host entertaining friends and passersby is still the rule. In the larger pubs much the same intimacy may prevail, at least toward the regulars. Still, the strict stereotype is dead, if indeed there ever were many such landlords. In all my travels I only met one publican who fit the image at all well and even he was too svelte; curiously, his cheery manner belied a deep pessimism about pubs, his town, Great Britain, and the rest of the world.

The brewers try to hire married couples as tenants at most pubs, to spread the heavy load of work, but also in recognition of the host role of the publican. Few tenants are single males. In a highly publicized case during the field work, a young woman who wanted to be a tenant advertised for a mate in an effort to meet brewers' specifications that she be married. Breweries do not seem to show a similar preference in managers, who are mostly in the very large houses and hotels anyway; many are single men and women.

Publicans are increasingly striving to maintain what the Morning Advertiser and other trade literature refer to as a businesslike manner. Most brewers and the Licensed Victuallers' association, or at least the editors of the

Morning Advertiser, feel that an air of efficiency is appropriate where business is transacted, and that the customers prefer this quality in a landlord. Cordiality is still desired, but as part of an image of a businessman providing maximum service. Managers, who are salaried employees, as opposed to tenants working on a "tied" contract, are often formally trained by the larger breweries, and, needless to say, not to be "mine jovial host."

Most publicans and their hired staff, if any, occupy roles and exhibit demeanor somewhere between the two extremes. In a quiet room their relationship with the patrons may be very much like that of the small pub's landlord. One example was that of the "Cocktail Bar" of the Lion Hotel, Fenston, in which a succession of three barmaids, all traveling Australians, found themselves giving solace or just listening to a regular clique of farmers who came in on Sunday afternoons and occasional other times, staking out the space immediately in front of the short bar counter.

In a busy room the staff may still maintain a special relationship with a certain group of regulars. At one place the barmaids frequently drank after hours with these patrons.

At the other end of the scale would be a barmaid who worked both bar counter and tables in the very large lounge

of a Bolton pub. She was noted for her libido-raising hot
pants suits and a figure of like effect. She flirted
constantly with male patrons, but always for a moment only,
then off she would go. She was therefore more
entertainment than acquaintance, from the standpoint of the
patrons more one of "them" than "us," male fantasies
nothwithstanding. The reactions of wives and girl friends
was indicative of this; they were more amused than jealous.
Casual flirting in cozier surroundings has brought down
wrath on many barmaids.

PUB SYSTEMS

The two preceding chapters outlined tradition and change
in pub design and clientele, leaving for now the tasks of
describing the trends in pub activities and synthesizing the
whole pattern of change within the systems model. This
chapter opens with trends in pub conversation and
entertainment, then moves on to describe the systems that
ought to be crucial in any discussion of pub change.

TRENDS IN PUB USE

Conversation

Drinking aside, conversation is the pub's <u>raison d'etre</u>.
Excepting the loners, pubgoers spend most of their time
chatting. That much does not change, and very likely the
topics discussed do not change much either. Apart from the
frequency of political discussion, Mass-Observation's
findings on topics and my own vary little. What does change
are the settings in which conversation takes place.

The spread of lounges, where people converse over small
tables, makes groups more private, participation less

communal. The net result is a steady decline in the number
of pubs or pub settings which serve as centers where
information and ideas are communicated that are significant
for more people than the patrons of that particular house.
Conversation in most traditional pub settings involves
everyone in the setting at least peripherally, and most of
what is said is to a degree community property. Lounge
conversation does not so often reach far across the room, an
observation borne out repeatedly in the field. Attendance is
also a factor. Nearly empty rooms of any type encourage
longer distance conversation, very crowded rooms permit very
little, while at intermediate patron densities the contrast
between lounges and many other settings is most evident.
Pubs are increasingly becoming places in which cliques
collect and act out their separate spheres of interactions,
notwithstanding local variation in how far the process has
gone.

Field observations showed a tendency for cliques to be
more isolated within the lounges. The cozier settings
allowed the most interaction between persons disparate in
their social memberships and associations, of differing ages,
for example. A few close settings, most of all the one and
two room pubs of Fenston, induced people to socialize with
individuals they avowedly dislike, an effect whose
desirability is arguable but also beside the point. What is

significant is that trends in pub design are making pub
society less inclusive.

The effects of other design changes parallel those of the
development of the lounge. For one thing, where the lounge
had complemented the smaller rooms, and the same people
inhabited all settings on a regular basis, now the lounge is
the pub to a large proportion of its patrons. Bar counters
are also being lengthened in all rooms, more tables provided
in public bars, and intrusive features such as fruit (slot)
machines installed.

Patron Self-Entertainment

Games on the whole have held their own in recent years,
but some that are special to particular regions may be on
their way out. The old standbyes; darts, dominoes, and
cribbage; are thriving and are found in some purportedly
unlikely settings. Contary to the opinions of several
publicans and at least one brewer that these games are
inappropriate to posh (in the minds of their planners)
establishments, field observations in the center of the City
of London found them prevalent in pubs that draw a well
heeled clientele.

Darts have emerged as the most played pub game. The
games that have lost the most ground have been those that are
ambitious undertakings played out of doors, in particular
pigeon racing and bowls. The holiday outings described by

Mass-Observation (1970:284-291) and by older Bolton informants commonly entailed advance planning and involved large numbers of participants, but they are now gone from most pubs, either in Bolton or anywhere else I went. Among outdoor games, the best survivor is fishing; organized matches and tournaments are still held in much of England. The rule, however, is that pub activities have retreated indoors.

Game trends parallel those of pub conversation. The games that best thrive today are those that require only a few players. Darts can be highly public, as in the News of the World tournaments, but most games are among small groups of friends. Pigeon racing in its heyday was not a public event, but at least it took in a broad cross section of the regulars at any pub. Large group affairs have suffered the greatest decline. Group activites can still be organized, and interpub darts and dominoes matches flourish across England, but in any given community the diversity and frequency of pub outings are less now than in times remembered by older patrons. In Bolton, where a few pubs sponsor fishing days, the range and frequency of these events was less than that detailed by Mass-Observation.

Patrons are today far less likely than formerly to provide their own music. Group sings were the rule before the second world war, but are the exception today; only two of the 83 pubs in the primary and secondary samples held

regular sings. The custom survives better in some parts of
the country, as I observed in rural Cumberland and was told
elsewhere, but the nationwide decline is dramatic. When
sings are held, a hired piano player or member of the staff
accompanies the singers. Today pianos are being removed at a
rapid rate, from most Bolton and Fenston pubs in the ten
years prior to the study. Other pianos go unused, or the
player has become more entertainer than accompanist. In the
one pub in the Bolton sample that held regular sings, a
microphone had been installed three or four years before, and
patrons' solos made up most of the singing.

    Why has the sing nearly disappeared? The trend follows
that noted for conversation and games, namely, a
privatization of all activity, but more explanation is
requisite, since the decline of sings has been rapid, yet the
ones I witnessed, most of them during brief visits on the
road, drew enthusiastic crowds of participants. Many
pubgoers, some of them young, were nostalgic. Darts matches
and "pay out" nights can still be arranged, and sings should
not be that much harder to keep going.

    The fact that only two pubs in the primary or secondary
samples held regular sings makes it difficult to pinpoint
what, if anything, accounts for their persistence in a few
pubs and their demise in so many more. The content of the
sings and peoples' perceptions of them nevertheless offer
some clues.

Regardless of the singers' ages, the songs heard during
the study were very much the same as those sung before the
war, songs most unlike the popular music of the 1950's and
1960's, very little of which lends itself to piano-chorus
arrangements. The old songs are mostly sentimental - "God
bless you and keep you, Sweet Mother Machree" - and the odd
one calls for participation - "You do the hokey pokey and you
turn yourself around, that's what it's all about," - but all
have lyrics far removed from "I can't get no satisfaction"
and other 1960's pop hits. A few singers at the King Alfred,
Fenston, tried a few Elvis Presley ballads (Presley was very
popular with the patrons, old and young), but the difficulty
of reproducing that modern musical commodity, the sound,
results in the music sounding less than right. Participants
at the King Alfred would always quickly return to the old
favorites. The patrons who took the microphone at the Bolton
pub mentioned above sang, or attempted to sing, country and
western songs or slower 1950's ballads, rather than the usual
fare of group sings, showing again that the more modern music
is hard to replicate.

The sings at the King Alfred, held Saturday nights but
somewhat irregularly, were successes by any measure except
profits. That is, regulars, occasional patrons, and
strangers took part, and the pub appeared busy and
flourishing, yet the receipts were not appreciably greater on
sing nights than on other Saturday nights, certainly not

enough greater to cover the piano player's free beers and
clear an extra profit. The landlord and landlady admitted
that they call in the piano player, an old friend, as much
for their own enjoyment as for any other reason.

Periodically, and in a variety of places, I heard of
patrons arranging diverse sorts of entertainment, from the
playing of traditional folk instruments to wrestling matches,
the latter in the Lakes country, but most of these events
turned out to be things of the past. The clientele of the
great majority of pubs do not initiate formal entertainment
on any regular basis. They have allowed a past function to
lapse: "The blokes what come in here are just apathetic
anymore. You can't stir them up to do anything now. Know
what I mean" (a Bolton publican)?

Entertainment Provided by the House

Over the postwar years the pubs have rapidly expanded and
developed the entertainment that the house provides. The low
point of provided entertainment may actually have come during
the early decades of this century. Eighteenth and nineteenth
drinking places, at least those in the "Grander than Home"
line, sponsored ratting, bear baiting, music, live dancing
shows, and more. This does not fault the comparison between
the 1930's and today, even if the 1930's were atypical in the
longer historical view.

The distinction between this sort of entertainment and that provided by the patrons is rarely blurred, usually quite easy to draw. A piano player at a sing is supplied by the house, and many events classed above as patrons' self entertainment are arranged by the tenant or manager, but the burden of keeping things going still falls on the participants.

In spite of sporadic and mostly futile attempts to introduce drama, poetry, and other varied titbits of "culture" into pubs, music is by far the dominant medium of provided entertainment. Besides pianos, organs have come in, though they reportedly peaked in the early 1950's and have since lost ground. Professional vocalists with accompanists, on the model of music hall singers, also gained and lost a pub following. Small bands of electric guitars, electric organs, drums, and group vocals appeared in numbers in the 1960's. The Beatles started on the pub circuit and were in this far from alone among groups of the time. The music heard in the study was not all rock; many groups played a potpourri tailored to the audience: Irish ballads, polkas, sentimental favorites, and other styles. Country and western had made recent inroads, especially in those Bolton pubs that catered to people of Irish background. The players came complete with cowboy hats and related paraphernalia.

Live music, while an attraction to nearly all pubgoers, is found in a minority of pubs outside of resort areas. In

Fenston only the <u>Lion Hotel</u> provided live music on a regular basis, although two other houses followed suit on odd occasions. Of the 42 pubs of the primary and secondary samples in Bolton, a half dozen had regular live music, mostly on weekends. Live music was most common in city center houses and was scattered fairly evenly throughout the rest of the city. Informants and my own observations both indicated that Bolton has more live music than most other urban centers. Fenston appears representative of smaller communities, although some rural and village pubs draw patrons from a distance by providing regular live music.

Jukeboxes supply the largest proportion of pub music across England as a whole, but their distribution is very uneven. In some places they are restricted to pubs that seek a young clientele, while in others they are ubiquitous, and people of all ages put money into them. Jukeboxes appeared in pubs during the 1950's, but gained a major role only in the 1960's. They thus parallel the development of live bands, not too surprisingly since much the same music is found in the machines as is played live. Jukeboxes are not necessarily so intrusive into other activities. While live music is nearly always loud enough to command undivided attention or at least wash out other activities, pubs vary greatly in how loudly the jukeboxes are played and how dominating are their locations.

Jukeboxes are most commonly located in a room of the lounge bar type, but can turn up in any conceivable sort of setting. Some of the newer pubs are designed with them specifically in mind; as a rule, the lounge is wholly or partly divided, and the jukebox is in one of the sections. The music that dominates one section is only background in the other.

"Canned" music, constant but inobtrusive, is not entertainment in the strictest sense and is not meant to be. It requires no participation, either, and no one really listens. While the music can serve as a background for many normal pub activities, including conversation at close quarters, it would be out of place in a setting where talk goes back and forth at some distance. "Canned" music is usually encountered in large lounges, often in those with especially pretentious decor, settings designed less for communal interaction than for small groups who keep to themselves.

"Canned" music actually declined rapidly after a certain vogue in the early 1960's. To brewery representatives it was an example of a passing fad, and I question how well it fits into pub life. The growing popularity of jukeboxes and live entertainment may also have aided its passing.

The incidence of television in pubs particularly varies from one place to another. "Tellies" are generally more common in the North than the South, but regional differences

are less significant than local variation. Sets are often
ubiquitous in the pubs of one town, nearly absent from the
next. Though all televisions are licensed in Great Britain,
no separate statistics are kept for those issued to pubs.
Out of the field sample, most sets were put in during the
1960's - I made a point of inquiring - but the rate of new
installations appears to be slowing down. The vast majority
of publicans turn them on only for selected programs. Sport
events usually take up most of the viewing time and are the
favorites nearly everywhere; many publicans and patrons
expressed the feeling that anything else is inappropriate in
their pub.

"Fruit" machines ("slot" machines in North America)
appeared after the Gaming Act of 1963. They too are very
common in some localities, but very unevenly distributed.
Playing them can be a sociable activity, but lone patrons,
either regular lone drinkers or those who are temporarily
alone, play them the most. Unlike darts, which also attract
lone players and groups, fruit machines rarely engender
competition. As a rule the players are almost as passive as
if they were dropping their coins into a jukebox. If
anything, jukeboxes involve the players more with other
patrons, since other patrons often help choose the song.

Other latecoming amusements include pinball, billiard
tables, "American" pool, and table football (soccer).
Occasionally a whole room is devoted to these games. Three

Bolton pubs did so, none in Fenston. These games are variously suited to lone players or to competition, but on the whole their installation appears to be a response to the needs of casual pubgoers, and they are not becoming established foci of collective interest in the manner of darts or cribbage boards.

The trend in pub activities is unmistakable over the past two decades. Down are those activities which center on the regulars or that otherwise tend to require interaction beyond one's immediate companions. Up are those which make no such demand. The shift is gradual, and anything lone patrons or couples do in pubs can also be a group activity; I recall one pub in which the older regulars accompanied nearly everything they did, including cribbage, by playing the jukebox. These allowances notwithstanding, gradual change has gone on long enough that the cumulative effect is anything but subtle. The trend is glaringly evident in virtually every pub that has in recent years been built or undergone major alterations or additions.

Advocates of and apologists for current pub change, among whom are numbered many of the licensing magistrates and spokespersons for the brewers and the Licensed Victuallers' Association, insist that most of the changes in pubs accomodate the two most rapidly growing sectors of the clientele: young singles and married couples. Many of the changes - increasingly passive entertainments are only part of the picture - allow pubs to be used more like cinemas or band concerts than alehouse kitchens. The tenor of facilities catering for married couples was set by the "improved public house" movement, but examples are to be found in which industry marketers anticipate this sort of demand and become tastemakers in the process.

THE SYSTEMS AND PUB TRENDS

Argument over where the pub is going turns not only on the use and design of pubs, but also on a host of symbols, for example, new tastes in drinks and changes in decor that are targeted at particular clienteles. The systems model now becomes useful to describe concurrent change in such diverse but integrated phenomena as activities, clientele, space, furnishings, and associated symbols.

The systems are named for some recurrent or especially significant feature, the clientele when that is consistent. The names are intended to be as descriptive as possible but cannot be inclusive. Though the youth system is unmistakably a set of things done by young patrons or with them in mind, appropriate settings are in English pubs rarely their exclusive territory, as in the 3.2 beer clubs of some States.

The list of systems does not exhaust the in which patrons, their use of pubs, and the physical features of pubs are integrated, but those systems that are prominent, prevalent, and especially well integrated are given. Some

other plausible systems, though perhaps significant, cannot
be described so economically. For example, a public bar
system is defensible, one that takes in the classic form of
the public bar and its casual use by workingmen, but in my
experience this kind of use is very diverse in its
traditional settings, and adaptable to some radically
disparate settings. The more cohesive regulars' system is
therefore used instead as a benchmark of change and
persistence and tradition.

The Youth System

An increase of young patrons in English pubs has been
accompanied by the crystallization of a distinct system.
Youths acting within the system behave in a fashion distinct
from that of other patrons, and settings that signal a young
clientele help attract those patrons. Young people have been
coming to pubs for a long time, and even today many join in
with older patrons in settings that are not especially
characteristic of the youth system, but the system is a
recognizable postwar development, one the industry nurtures.

No age category but the young is so associated with its
own symbols or holds forth over so much of its own space.
Some things have connotations of other age categories, for
example, playing dominoes while wearing a heavy overcoat and
sipping pints of mild ale, but these associations are not so

numerous and not generally so strong as those that surround
youth.

Contrary to cliches that would have them forever
partying, young people concentrate by far the greatest part
of their pub time in small conversational groups. When in
groups, particularly in mixed groups and in large pubs, young
patrons are mainly to be found in the lounges. This was
particularly true in Bolton. In the public bars and older
style, cozier settings, young pubgoers socialize freely with
patrons of other ages, and not just with a tight clique of
age mates. Participation in the youth system thus fits most
naturally into a setting which affords the small group some
privacy and autonomy, logically enough, the lounge.

Lounges are not often the exclusive territory of the
young. Only a few serve them to the near exclusion of other
patrons. Fenston had two which saw few clients past thirty.
In Bolton one "club;" by any accepted definition really a
vast, multilevel pub; was strictly a youth hangout, but
otherwise the young crowd dominated only scattered small
settings. Bolton appears typical of the urban North, in that
young patrons stake claim to only a section or corner of the
odd lounge.

The youth system is more often set apart by its wealth of
symbols than by physical boundaries or the exclusion of other
patrons. Participants tend to dress differently than when
they join their fathers for a darts match after work or their

mothers for a round of stout. The drinks differ as well,
particularly for the young women; I met several who made it a
point to order one drink at a local and another when out with
a young crowd. The latter drinks are usually costlier,
something not lost on the trade's advertisers: "Don't let him
buy you off with a bottle of stout. Tell him you want a
Baby-Cham."

Though a sizeable minority of young marrieds take part,
the system bears the mark of mating and dating. The
possibility of meeting members of the opposite sex draws
singles, but few actually pair off there. The primary sample
took in four pub rooms with especially large numbers of
single women among the clientele, mostly 18-20 years old.
Although most who regularly went to the pub had at one time
or another left with a male they met there or arranged for a
date at another time, few did so at all often. All the same,
awareness that one may meet someone may be read in the
uneasiness of some younger participants and the studied
indifference of many older ones. That certain pubs acquire a
widespread reputation as meeting places and attract a
particularly young clientele bears witness to the drawing
power of that reputation. Given the dearth of actual
pairings, it would be interesting to know how the reputation
was acquired in the first place, but little explanation can
be offered apart from location, say, near a university. Male
informants in Lancashire repeatedly told me that one mill

town has pubs that are a "great place to pick up a bird." A
Saturday night visit confirmed that in some city center
houses an unusual number of men and women left with a member
of the opposite sex that they met there, but from one visit
it was impossible to determine previous acquaintance, if any.

Music is a very common accompaniment, but it is more the
method of listening and in many places the intrusiveness of
the music that sets off the system. Listening is itself no
monopoly of the young. Regulars play the jukebox. So did
one business executive, a patron of local arts societies,
alomost daily at a local pub during the lunch hour. Live and
recorded music are so prevalent in Bolton that they must take
in all ages. But music is certainly more dominant within the
youth system than without, and it is indispensable in many
settings catering to young patrons.

The role of music in the youth system is symptomatic of
the way in which other activities, few of them the exclusive
province of the young, become critical elements of that
system and acquire minor nuances that convey their
association with youth. The young listen to music the most
and have their own style of listening, or better, of moving
to the music, and they move with more enthusiasm when with
their peers in appropriate surroundings than they do when
they join the regulars at a neighborhood local. The argot of
the young also comes out more within the youth system.

Goffman's (1959) stage metaphor is apposite, the suggestion that people act out roles appropriate to the theater of the moment. To force his metaphor a bit, the pub, or part of it, is the stage, but the system is the play. The subtle changes in role and style enacted by the youth system's actors, the young patrons, when they enter the stage and join the play maintain the identity of the system.

Of the symbols most strongly associated with the youth system, some, like certain pairing behavior and styles of dress, are common to youth in other public theaters, while others are more specific to youth in pubs, including "pop" motifs in the wallpaper and mixed drinks of vodka and fruit juice. A few symbols signal particular subsystems: motorcycle jackets and wall portraits of Cambridge sports teams.

An exhaustive list of associated symbols and features would be too long to attempt, but examples will be given how some are manipulated to mold clientele and usage, first with three case histories that illustrate well the workings of the youth system. The first two, from Fenston, trace the effects of installing a jukebox. A young crowd almost wholly replaces the previous, older clientele of one pub, but the result in the other is minor in spite of frequent playing. The third case, from Bolton, demonstrates a loose association of certain symbols with particular variants or subsystems of the youth system.

The replacement of older patrons took place in the
"Lounge Bar" of the Lion Hotel, shown in Figure 10. The
hotel has overnight guests and also features a "Cocktail Bar"
across the hall.

The "Lounge Bar" decor is not especially plush, but a
carpet, wallpaper, comfortably upholstered chairs, and
polished wood tables give the room an appearance of enhanced
status. The "Cocktail Bar," a bit smaller room, has a
shorter bar counter, and more expense is evident in the decor
and the furniture, which is arranged on a lounge plan.

Both rooms were originally intended for a middle class
clientele. The present building dates to the early years of
this century, when an outbuilding housed the "Lion Tap," in
its function a classic public bar for the working class
trade. The "Tap" was closed about 1954. At that time the
"Cocktail Bar" catered mainly to hotel guests, the "Lounge
Bar" to local businessmen and farmers, in particular on
market days, when the town center pubs were (and are) allowed
to remain open through the normal afternoon closing hours.
Both trades have fallen off since then, the drinking by the
hotel guests in line with a nationwide trend among motoring
travelers. The farmers, along with a lesser number of hotel
guests, young professionals and business apprentices, became
the mainstay of the "Cocktail Bar." Townspeople and a few
guests, a mostly older crowd, took over the "Lounge Bar,"

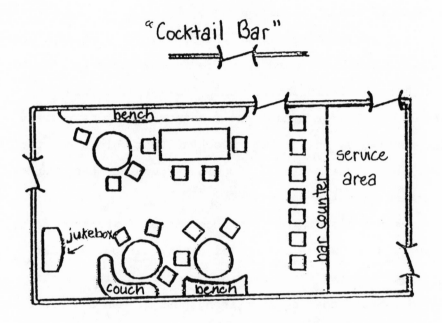

Figure 10. The "Lounge Bar," <u>Lion Hotel</u>, Fenston

filling the room on market days, but providing a dwindling trade the rest of the week.

While the "Cocktail Bar" remained profitable by drawing on what had been the clientele of both rooms, the "Lounge Bar" was not, and became on all but market days a place to sit at small tables and converse in low tones and in small groups with little interference from other patrons. Unfortunately for management receipts shrank as privacy grew. Interestingly, only in the "Cocktail Bar" did a group of regulars make a habit of crowding around the bar counter chatting with the barmaid.

The hotel's dining room accomodated fewer townspeople than guests. While patrons of either bar could order food from the counter staff, a display of food like that so often found in pubs that do a thriving businessmen's lunch trade was missing.

The effect of the lounge's jukebox, installed shortly before my observations began, is not hard to imagine. Empty spaces and pervasive quiet ceased as a young crowd began to filter in and drop coins, at first on market afternoons and then most evenings. The former customers left. All but the odd hotel guest stuck to the "Cocktail Bar."

The jukebox sufficed to bring about the change. No design changes were needed, and in general the ingredients for the youth system were already there. The barmaids were young, attractive, and vivacious. The same lounge plan that

accomodated that complex mixture of cliques and elbow rubbing
that so often characterizes settings popular with a young
crowd. The noise, the inevitable jam at the bar counter, and
a jukebox played constantly at high volume, generated the
appropriate atmosphere.

The managers by their account and that of the staff and
some patrons intended the changes wrought by the jukebox.
The effect was sweeping because it produced changes in an
environment that could not be part of two so irreconcilable
systems.

Jukebox installation in the other Fenston example had no
such radical effect. Figure 11 shows the licensed area. One
design feature in particular bears upon what took place; the
snall, half separated space in the rear allows a fair degree
of quiet when the jukebox is played. The volume is rarely
high, though the publicans sometimes have to stop enthusiasts
(not always young) from turning it up.

This pub is very much a local, though some patrons today
drive from remote parts of Fenston. The clientele is
heterogeneous in several respects. Mainly a blue collar pub,
it nevertheless draws quite a few middle class customers,
usually long term Fenston residents. All ages of legal
drinkers are well represented. Several pairs of fathers and
sons frequent the _Alfred_. Women take part in everything the
regulars normally do, including cribbage tournaments and
darts teams, and serve as officers in the pub clubs. That

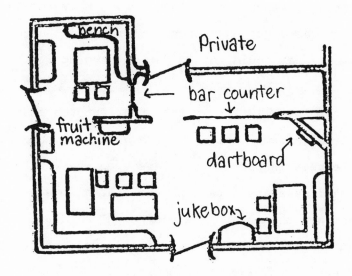

Figure 11.   The King Alfred, Fenston

much female participation is found in one other Fenston pub,
but in the remainder a few activities are at least _de facto_
male prerogatives or specialities.

The _Alfred_ is often congested on Saturday nights and
Sunday afternoons, but ten to fifteen customers is the norm
at other peak hours. A number of the male regulars come in
daily at the noon hour and again in the evening, and are
personal friends of the landlady (the tenant of record) and
landlord. With the other regulars they constitute the bulk
of the trade, but occasional customers and one time visitors
are fairly common.

About a year before the field work a local group of young
people began to frequent the pub and rather openly use drugs,
principally sundry pills. Needless to say, they did not
drink a lot of beer, but they did drive away the regulars.
With a little assist from the police the present tenants
chased away this crowd, and every one of the regulars
returned.

These same tenants subsequently installed the jukebox.
The effect was to draw a few more young patrons, but none of
those added became a frequent visitor. Nor did any older
regulars stay away, almost constant play at peak hours
notwithstanding. In fact the regulars play a good proportion
of the songs. Though the patron's age has its effect on the
songs he or she is most likely to play, that selection still
must be made from the same set of hit singles that is in

nearly every other pub. The presence of the jukebox poses
the questions why it does not lure more young patrons and why
it interferes so little with the doings of the older
customers.

This pub simply does not provide an appropriate setting
for the youth setting. It is too small to provide either
separate space for little groups or cliques or the bustle and
noise that a large crowd generates. The layout is distinctly
sociopetal in its effect. It is hard to go there and not
take part, unless one takes on the lone drinker role. Young
people adjust their behavior to fit the _Alfred_; many also go
to the "Lounge Bar" at the _Lion Hotel_, and on a number of
occasions I noticed changes in demeanor in groups going back
and forth. They would be isolated, even aloof, at the _Lion_,
but melt into the general round at the _Alfred_. This shift
often meant altering interaction with the same people,
because other groups would go between the two houses.

What will be described below as the regulars' system
dominates the _Alfred_. The high degree of integration of
activities of different ages and sexes makes this pub more
than most a "home from home" in which a great deal of time is
spent. Patrons mix diverse activities and cannot be as
single minded as those regulars who formerly sought quiet
conversation in the "Lounge Bar" of the _Lion_, and unlike the
latter they were able to adapt to the jukebox.

Tenants and regulars at the <u>Alfred</u> made some
accomodations, but also worked out rules that would minimize
the impact of the jukebox on customary activities. Rules
govern its playing: never when a darts or dominoes league
match is going on or on the odd Saturday nights when the
piano player comes in. This pub's regulars include an inner
core and a larger group. The difference is mainly one of
personal relationships with the tenants. The inner core gets
together frequently, usually late on a busy night, to toss
around a lot of jokes and some unusually personal
conversation, and the tenants take part as time permits. At
these times they nearly always retreat to the rear space,
where the sound of the jukebox is muted.

Specific scenarios that follow jukebox introduction are
presumably highly varied, but at least in Bolton's locals the
outcome has more often been like Fenston's <u>Alfred</u> than the
<u>Lion</u>. Most of Bolton's locals are large by Fenston
standards, and their greater capacity permits more segregated
activities and jukebox playing without too much invasion of
the more distant nooks and crannies. Older patrons play the
jukebox at many houses and carry on other activities as well.
Jukeboxes are not always introduced into neighborhood locals
with minimal disturbance, however. Two brewers'
representatives related instances in which the action routed
the established patrons, and I found many pubs, including
some in Bolton, whose regulars were aghast at the suggestion.

Regulars' systems and their locals vary greatly. Some can
adapt to a jukebox and some cannot, and I believe the
difference is fairly predictable on a case-by-case basis.
The effect of this or any other innovation must be weighed
against not only who the customers are but also what they do
in that particular setting.

In the third case history, from Bolton, symbols were
seemingly manipulated to allot different young clientele to
specific settings. A jukebox was only one of the
innovations. At first glance the division is between working
class and middle class, contrasts in decor following
stereotypes of class preference, but on closer examination
the corresponding division in the clientele, though real, was
not so distinct as first thought.

The pub, the <u>Black Bear</u>, was on a side street near the
city center. Figure 12 shows the plan.

The area on the left (looking from the street) along the
bar counter is a fairly typical regulars' citadel. Rather
austere in its amenities and decor, it is a small base for a
surprisingly large number of regulars, nearly all men over
thirty years of age. They use dominoes equipment a great
deal at slack periods. At peak hours they maintain a
remarkably unified set of social interactions in very crowded
conditions.

This pub always had the one entrance. The room layout
and the placement of the bar counter are unchanged.

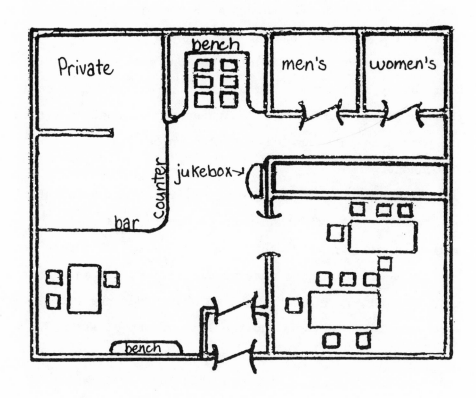

Figure 12.   The Black Bear, Bolton

Not so the functional divisions of the <u>Black Bear</u>'s
space: the tiny room (without a door) in the rear was,
judging from one informant's account, once the regulars'
citadel, dominated well into the 1950's by a group of elderly
men. The front left area and the central hall were then more
or less the classic public bar, the one physically divided
room, at right front, a ladies' room. Patrons still call
this last room the "parlor," although at present no titles
are posted in this pub; "best" room prices prevail
throughout.

The functional division was thus fairly representative,
on a small scale, of urban pubs in working class
neighborhoods and city center back streets. Clientele and
their use of space have changed since then, but mainly in the
tiny rear room. How, why, and in what order the alterations
were made is not known, and the lack of any clear
recollection on the part of a few old regulars may mean the
changes were gradual, not a dramatic turn accompanied by an
invasion of new customers. Whatever the chain of events, the
current clientele and use of space contrasts sharply with
what went before.

The central hall continues to serve as a small classic
public bar. Most casual visitors and occasional patrons
station themselves along the bar counter, and drinkers from
the rear room move back and forth with their orders; waitress
service is provided, but only at peak times. A jukebox in

the hall is audible throughout the pub but loudest in the rear room and the "parlor," owing to the placement of the speakers.

The "parlor" still draws its older women regulars, but has become a small lounge with a scant majority of young people among its clientele, a change brought about without any sweeping alteration of the design or decor. A carpet, the curtains, a couple of still life prints, and minor bits of decoration are new, but the six tables and the darts board are not. Darts are played quite a lot, and seats accomodate about twenty-five, giving the room an unclutered and broadly traditional look. While it once served as a ladies' room, it is just large enough to provide separate social settings, each focused on one or two of the tables, especially when crowded.

The appearance of most of the pub is plain but not austere, barely "best" room, but the rear room is another matter. Stucco and false oaken beams give the ceiling a Tudor effect. Horse brasses festoon the walls, also hung with an ornately framed neo-impressionist print. The wallpaper is scarlet and richly textured, reminiscent of some New Orleans Bourbon interiors, and a thick carpet dresses the floor. Six tiny tables crowd one another, and the upholstered oak benches that take up the three walls seat at most fifteen patrons. Not only is the setting intimate, getting in and out can be very difficult at peak hours.

This rear room is unusual, resembling more than anything
the alcoves being built into many of the new lounges. One
wonders for whom the renovations were originally intended.
Their total effect is overwhelmingly sociopetal, nearly to
the point that those in the setting must be on familiar
terms. Such an environment would necessarily be taken over
by a regular crowd on close terms with one another, yet would
be dysfuncytional for many of the traditional regulars'
activities, quite aside from the possible effect of the
decor.

While neither the rear room nor the right front room has
an appearance which would appeal only to a young crowd, the
social effect of their design and the proximity of the
jukebox help attract a young crowd. Both rooms are also
excellent places for conversation.

Three cliques of young people frequent the Black Bear,
and their activities and use of space fit the description of
the youth system. One dominates the rear room. The other
two gather mainly in the right front room. All of these
young patrons tend to gather at the bar counter when only a
few are in the pub, especially if they are males only, and
drift into the rooms as more of their compatriots come in.

The apparent class division is by room: middle class in
the rear, working class in the right front. The decor in the
"parlor" is in the tradition of a working class sitting room.
Several of the features of the rear room, though executed

with atypical ostentation, resemble those of many pubs that
attract a predominantly middle class clientele, including the
Tudor ceiling, horse brasses, oaken furniture, and the choice
of painting. The breakdown of the young clientele follows
suit enough that when I first observed this pub, I believed I
had found some oft encountered class differences in pub
preference represented in miniature.

Subsequent investigation showed the generalization to be
too neat. Much of the conversation in the rear room, for
instance about folk music or events at the local
technological institute, fits the stereotype, and most of the
frequent patrons did turn out to be professionals, business
apprentices, or students pursuing higher education, but a few
manual workers were also included. A large proportion,
probably a majority, came from working class families. None
spoke anything approaching public school dialect.

The young cliques of the "parlor" are similarly mixed.
Most are working class, but a number of youths of white
collar occupation or background are also included.

The individuals concerned are probably unaware that their
preferences for one setting are more shared with one class
than another, whereas around the country class associations
were evident in pubs and pub settings frequented by youth.
The tendency is evident in the makeup of the clientele, but,
in agreement with general principles of probability and
sampling, is not always so evident in each pub. Regarding

the Black Bear, it would be worth knowing if the remodeling
was intended, to produce the social effects noted, but the
publican who made the changes was no longer within reach.

The Bistro System

The title, a metaphor with European establishments which
more than pubs have a tradition of small tables and intimate
conversation, refers to a system that centers in the lounge,
where it meets others, notably the youth system. The two
systems overlap in their frequent use of lounges and the
prevalence of semiprivate conversations, though conversations
in the bistro system tend to be the more private. The tone
of the bistro system is set by married couples on evenings
out together, just as mating and dating behavior (even if
more potential than real) shape so much of the youth system.

The bistro system is not so replete with its own
distinctive features as the youth system. The decor of the
lounges drawing older patrons is less stereotyped, the
atmosphere more varied from pub to pub and town to town.
Apart from a conducive room plan, no single purveyance is
likely to have a singular effect drawing the appropriate
clientele, the way a jukebox may draw young patrons.

In spite of this diversity, the bistro system is
identifiable in pubs all over England, and its growth is a
key part of pub change. People take part in the system

mainly as couples, either sitting alone or congregating in
small conversational groups. That much is not new, but only
recently has such use of pubs become so prevalent that
specialized settings are widely created for its accomodation,
so much so in fact that this use appears more than any other
to be accomodated in new designs. Conventions of behavior
have also jelled around this growing use of pub space, fully
justifying the depiction of a distinct pub system.

Men have long joined their wives in the ladies' rooms and
lounges of traditional pubs, but for the most part the sexes
played their roles separately, most of all at those hours
when social interaction was at a peak. Even in the small,
cozy, backstreet pubs, exemplified by several in Fenston, and
despite the acceptance of women into the regulars' citadels
of many, the practice has long prevailed whereby the landlady
retreats with the married women into her sitting room or
another licensed room. In some parts of the country women
once stayed out of all parts of the pubs.

The ladies' room is today a dying feature. In Fenston
the pubs that retain it are the very ones slated to be shut
down in the near future. The removal of room dividers from
large pubs around England casts everyone into the lounges.

Many men are still able to divide their time; in Bolton
especially men commonly spend a weekday evening or two with
their "mates" in the citadel of their local and the public
bars of this and other houses, then join their wives in the

lounge on weekends. However, the bistro system is robust and
growing, something evident whether one counts the couples
among the clientele of the lounges or notes the proliferation
of facililties for their use.

The kind of social use that characterizes this system is
found outside of lounges, and in addition, groups other than
couples sometimes make parallel use of lounges. Still, the
heart of the system, and something well known to people
involved with pubs and pub change, is the use of lounges by
married couples.

The appropriate decor is that which contributes to an
effect that participants are given to calling "nice." The
features so described are variable and, being less
stereotyped than those of some other systems, allow much room
for individual creativeness. "Niceness" is most evident in
contrast to the bare walls and dark wood surfaces of male
dominated settings. The decor suggests at least moderate
expense, an impression that may be quite superficial, based
on the addition of furnishings available at modest cost from
some discount distributors, while conversely the odd
furnishings of some public bars have over the years acquired
an antique value, but the impression is no less real for
that, and informants frequently noted with approval
publicans' expenditures in making rooms "nice."

Modernness is also much sought after, and an effect
reminiscent in some respects of home sitting rooms, yet a bit

austere. Critics have likened the final appearance to an
airport waiting room, perceiving only the austerity, but on
the other side furniture tends to follow current home styles,
emphasizing light pieces and textures, while little touches
such as potted plants and flower print wallpaper add to the
sitting room look. These warmer qualities are perhaps most
manifest in urban pubs located away from city centers or in
new housing estates.

A contrasting approach to lounge decor is to follow a
rustic architectural theme. Most often this is done in
keeping with the whole pub, and frequently following some
historical claim to the style, though isolated Tudor lounges
are to be found. When the whole pub follows some period
style the expense is likely to be well over the average for a
lounge. The bistro system then remains a possible use, but
repaying the cost demands a high turnover, at least at
certain hours, thus working against the moderate degree of
quiet and privacy that typifies the system. Pubs with a "bit
of history" are therefore often places where the bistro
systems meets the businessmen's lunch system or the youth
system. Two or three of these systems may share the same
space at different hours.

Well lit rooms for "family" use are a legacy of the
"improved public house" movement. Temperance reformers
equated dark rooms with sinister goings on, a judgement that
may have carried over into the "improved public house"

movement and beyond. Interestingly the reverse applies in
the United States, where lounges frequented by couples tend
to be kept dim, the neighborhood taverns brightly lit. Most
English pubgoers, when asked, expressed indifference to the
amount of lighting, and no reason is apparent to second guess
informants on this score and impute a subliminal effect.
Whatever the reason for the bright lights, they are a normal
part of the bistro system, though likely dispensable.

Participants dress in a manner deemed appropriate to the
system, though not one that is mandatory. Men who wear
trousers, an old shirt, and a rough coat to the regulars'
citadel often don a suit and tie to join their wives in the
lounge. On older men the suits are often baggy sorts that
they have worn for years. Professional men may dress as they
would for work. The women too dress with extra care, but
well short of being formal, and in ways that are harder to
characterize in brief. Many young couples, the men and women
alike, follow current fashions when out together. Pubs that
enforce dress codes are thought pretentious in many quarters,
are found mainly in town centers, and often cater to a young
trade. Before the second world war dress rules may have
operated to exclude working class patrons, but such was not
the case anywhere that I visited, and would be unlikely now
that class differences in dress are less clear cut.

Rules of decorum specific to the system or at least more
pronounced in this context constrain behavior. Patent

intoxication is unacceptable, one sharp departure from the
etiquette of the youth system. Slightly different rounds
buying customs hold; the couple may take their turn as one
person. Collections of couples are less likely to invite in
newcomers than are many groups of regulars.

The sphere of interaction of pubgoers is reduced within
this system. Though couples often enough join with others,
the presence of one's partner appears within this context to
inhibit long range interaction across the lounge.

The Businessmen's Lunch System

A third system that is growing in visibility and
significance to the trade is the businessmen's lunch system,
though it is not as prevalent as the youth system or the
bistro system. Lunch is the raison d'etre, but convenience
to places of white collar employment and an appropriate menu
do not by themselves suffice to attract the requisite trade.
Potential patrons have come to expect distinctive
environmental features, many of them peculiar to pubs, and
not to be found in restaurants and cafes. Some categories of
patrons other than businessmen, university students for
example, patronize these same settings, but most often
facilities of this type have developed around a business
trade. "Businessmen" at the time of the study included some
businesswomen, a distinct minority, but not one which

appeared to be excluded by any social rules operating on the premises.

A prominent display of food, the "groaning board," is gaining in pubs, where it is already far more common than in other eating places. The sight evokes associations with past feasts of Olde England, and the inevitable roast beef occupies the place of honor. Service is usually over a side of the bar counter, dining less formal than in restaurants which cater to the same trade. Even the food, mostly sandwiches and salads, is more casual. "It's more relaxing, less bother," offered one Bolton businessman.

The archaic image of Ye Olde Inn may be carried one step further. I found four pubs in which Tudor decor had been built into a room at a time when extensive food service was set up for a luncheon trade, and others in which the trade and the decor similarly coincided, but the renovations could not be dated.

The space for this trade may be in a separate room, occasionally one that is open only at the noon hour, but more commonly in new and newly remodeled houses it is in an alcove off a lounge, space that reverts to other forms of lounge use during the evening hours. An example of the plan is shown in Figure 13, from a large Bolton center pub.

The furnishings usually reflect some expense, more than is typical of the bistro system, but seldom ostentation.

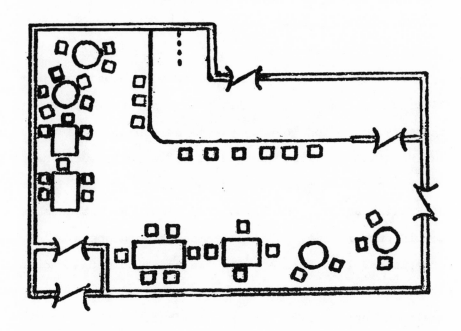

Figure 13. "Lounge" and Dining Area,
the <u>Beige Horse</u>, Bolton

The businessmen's lunch system is housed in "grander than home" but not "frankly theatrical" style. Some of the sites that most successfully draw the trade, particularly in Cambridge and the City of London, are decorated in masculine motifs: a lot of leather, oak, and dark colors, but on costlier, better kept up furnishings than those typical of the classic public bar.

Sales of food have increased in more pubs than just those fitting the preceding description, a point of pride with many industry spokesmen, but away from suitable locations for the business lunch trade, pubs still sell mostly such snacks as steak and kidney pies and bags of potato crisps. About 21% of English adults, roughly one-third of the pubgoers, ever eat in pubs (Cooper 1970:3). Among the pubgoers of my experience, less than a third ate anything often enough to be at all meaningful. Very few working class people take full meals in pubs unless they are residents in those few that offer accomodations. After a brewer's representative cited a pub on a council housing estate as one that did a booming trade in meals among a neighborhood clientele, I visited the pub, talked with the publican, and found the report completely in error; brewers would not ordinarily have records of food sales, which are a landlord's perquisite under most tenancy contracts. Many brewers are on record with plans to expand food service, even to include fish and

chips in a few houses, plans that are overambitious unless a
new and independent pattern of pub use can be brought into
being, one with a broader base of support than the
businessmen's lunch system.

The Regulars' System

Portions of previous chapters described the regulars and
the regulars' citadel. That these comprise the backbone of
the trade and a still prominent part of pub space justifies
the attention, but leaves perhaps the question why the
description of a regulars' system is not redundant. The
answer is that no other system better illustrates the
usefulness of dealing with change in a framework which
unifies actors and their environments. This system goes back
to the alehouse and is more than any other imbued with
tradition. It also proves to be a reference point for pub
change, one against which to judge the pub's place in English
society. The regulars' system is made up of the social rules
that govern the regulars and also of the characteristic
features of the regulars' citadels, but in sum these things
are greater than when taken separately.

The individual regulars' system is open ended, not
strictly bounded by the local. Nearly all regulars at one
pub visit others, many individuals and groups of mates are
regulars in more than one pub, and occasionally two or more

locals share nearly the same set of regulars. Somewhat
arbitrarily then I shall isolate particular pubs as case
studies, though an exchange can be assumed of patrons and
their ideas of atmosphere and decorum.

Environmental features are an integral part of the
system. Each participating group needs a setting that is
sociopetal, yet accomodates larger aggregates than the
couples and pairs of couples who keep the bistro system
going. It will be recalled from Chapter Four that both the
"mates" and the usual women's groups tend to collect at the
local on an informal basis; set or arranged times are the
exception. A cozy setting that they more or less dominate,
when they are present, is therefore a real convenience. Less
tangible qualities, the social environment rather than the
physical, also contribute to the feeling of "home from home."
As a Bethnal Green man put it, "I don't want to feel a
stranger where I go for a pint." Proper company and the
appropriate environment are thus mutually reinforcing
qualities.

Nonspatial features; i.e., decor, amenities, and styles
of furnishings; are less readily assessed for dispensability
or indispensability, though when former pub qualities are
recalled with nostalgia or criticism heaped on the new, in
ways that suggest adherence to the traditions of the
regulars' system, aesthetics are more often cited than floor

plan. Much of the talk within pubs about pubs is frankly
nostalgic, even among younger patrons, and occasionally the
press relates an instance in which the regulars of a pub take
strong exception to an aesthetic change. Certainly dark
colors, masculine motifs, and an overall impression of
simplicity and utility predominate in traditional male
dominated settings and have a high message value within the
regulars' system, but changes of decor and plan are so often
made together that it is hard to separate their impact. A
few relevant case histories can be offered from the field
study.

In one Fenston pub and another in the Bolton secondary
sample the regulars' system carried on undisturbed after
extensive remodeling. Though the alterations were made
during the three or four years preceding the field work,
these pubs continue to bear every mark of the local and draw
their most regular patrons from near at hand. Most of the
regulars go back several years before the renovations, and
their accounts of past use of the pubs were quite clear,
leaving no reason to doubt their judgement that alteration
had minimal social effect.

The Bolton case is probably the more pertinent, since the
renovations had a dramatic impact on atmosphere, but effected
little change in the allocation and division of space. Vinyl
seat covers, bright lights, linoleum, and other touches made
the appearance ostensibly modern. The one change in the

floor plan was the removal of a wall between the "Snug" and the "Public Bar," something that has not prevented the "Snug" keeping its function as a place for the inner circle of older regulars, and the rest of the house retains its previous neighborhood clientele and use.

The more drastic renovation was that of the Union Jack, Fenston, built from the ground up on the site of a very small neighborhood pub that had only one licensed room in regular use. It now has both a "Lounge" and a "Public Bar." The latter (Figure 14), follows a lounge plan, its title notwithstanding. Tables are dispersed, and openness, pastels, and bright colors set the mood. Yet it differs from the typical lounge. The tables are larger than average for lounges and are scattered along the walls, the usual arrangement in regulars' citadels in Fenston. This leaves a space in front of the darts board, and patrons make almost continuous use of the board and of dominoes equipment at the tables. At least three collections of regulars get together frequently in this room, groups that are on good terms with one another but interact more when few people are present than when the pub is crowded. Within the room several spaces are favorite haunts of particular groups. One group on particularly close terms with the landlord holds forth in the top right hand corner.

This pub and the remodeled Bolton house retained adequate provision for the regulars' system, and other pubs were found

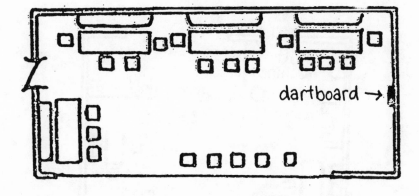

Figure 14.   "Public Bar," the Union Jack, Fenston

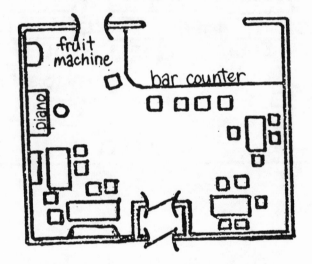

Figure 15.   "Lounge," the Corner Pub, Bolton

in which the regulars carried on traditional interaction and
activities in spaces whose decor was modern. It thus seems
that modern trappings per se are not necessarily incompatible
with the traditional regulars' system, and the brewers and
planners' concepts of modernity do not offend pubgoers enough
to force a change of locals, if indeed offence is felt at
all. Though it would always be wise to consult the regulars
before remodeling, something I did encounter and hear of, the
more drastic fears of some nostalgist writers probably
reflect more their own feelings than those of most patrons,
even including the older regulars.

Though the regulars' adherence to traditional aesthetics
has perhaps been overstated, the provision of a plan
conducive to their established activities is demonstrably
more essential. Above all the regulars require some
sociopetal space for a home base. Intensive observation of
pubs in the primary sample revealed that the most cohesive
groups, particularly those that include a core of members who
turn out several times a week, consistently have their
citadels in those pubs where they can take over some
particular space. Such groups tend to be found more in older
pubs that provide a "snug," "taproom," or other made to order
regulars' citadel, but the field work also uncovered some
seemingly inhospitable settings adapted by the regulars to
suit their purposes. Regulars were encountered that made use
of lounges as home bases. Alcoves or other cozy subdivisions

facilitate matters, but sometimes groups make a habit of
coming in at hours when sales are slow, when they can
maintain communication much as they would in a closer
setting. Figure 15 shows a Bolton lounge used by regulars in
this fashion.

Regulars gather here evenings between seven and eight,
and form a cohesive group, less perhaps than in most back
street pubs, but sufficiently to make this an adequate local.
The core of the group is on especially good terms with the
landlord, and on most evenings interaction focuses on a half
dozen or so men (with much turnover from night to night) at
the bar counter. Shouting back and forth involves them with
people at the tables: women's groups, mixed groups, and
regular loners for the most part. People move back and forth
to the fruit machine, exchanging bits of conversation along
the way.

As the evening passes the crowd becomes too dense to
allow easy interchange around the room. Interaction
disperses into small social groups seated at the tables and
in groups of one, two, or three people at the bar counter.
The exchanges involving patrons on their way to the fruit
machine dwindle to simple greetings.

One lesson of the Corner Pub is that regulars can adapt,
and this example, though the best from the field work, is not
the only one. The lesson should be qualified in several
ways. Internal unity is greatest where the local provides a

sort of clubhouse space, and a great many regulars express a
preference for such pubs, either directly referring to plans
of this type, or citing pubs that include them. Another
point, one that many discussions of the pub and tradition
miss, is that the regulars are mobile, only the oldest being
content to stay in their one local. Bolton men, when making
rounds with their "mates," use their local mainly as a
starting and finishing point, and frequently use different
pubs in distinctive ways. Some groups tour crowded public
bars and lounges to jam elbows amid a lot of noise and then
return to their local for the end of the evening ritual,
"Drink up, gentlemen." On Sunday they might well come back to
the local for dominoes. No one pub, no matter how well
designed, could provide as much variety as a tour of pubs,
and the regulars enjoy the moving about as much as anything
else.

The regulars' system, in the form that it presently
assumes in those urban neighborhoods that provide a variety
of pubs within walking distance, will survive any conceivable
changes in the design and management of pubs, because
pubgoers will continue to shop around for what suits them,
but will thrive only if the locals are satisfactory home
bases. The regulars'systems of small villages may or may not
operate very differently; it is here that the lack of
intensive field work in a rural community is most felt.

Which traditional activities are crucial, which features

so alien and intrusive that their addition causes a change in
the whole round of activities? Again the individuality of
each setting has to be taken into account. Recall the
discussion of the youth system and the two pubs contrasted
for the impact of jukeboxes. Two more cases will now present
a contrast in the vitality and resilience of the regulars'
system in particular pubs. In one the regulars have adapted
well to a potentially intrusive feature, while in the other
the system is disintegrating. The first case involves the
introduction of a television set. Details are lacking about
the pub prior to installation, said to have been anywhere
from two to five years before the field work, but the
publican is the same, and reportedly the clientele has turned
over only slightly. The main drinking room is shown in
Figure 16. The one other licensed room was formerly often
used by the landlady to entertain women regulars, but is
rarely opened today.

Nearly all the patrons are regulars; despite a location
on a major thoroughfare near the town center few casual
visitors are to be seen. Most of the regulars are also
regulars at one or two other Fenston houses, and their
average age is rather high, well over forty years. The
publican and his wife are on close terms with all of them and
chat back and forth with everyone present when they are not
too busy.

Few of the regulars spend the entire evening at the Royal

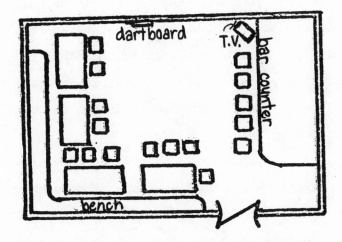

Figure 16.   Main room, the <u>Royal Arms</u>, Fenston

Arms, although many finish there; the pub does not fill until
the last hour. Group activities are not so varied as in the
other Fenston locals, for example the King Alfred, with which
many of the regulars are shared. One group of old age
pensioners is the exception, eight men who spend a great deal
of time there both mornings and evenings. Though all
wandered more when younger, they now rarely drink anywhere
else. At least four are usually present except during the
early evening hours, always seated at the table to the left
of the door. They play dominoes almost constantly, and at
times the landlord or a regular outside the clique join in to
make a foursome.

This is the only pub in Fenston with television, and
unlike the sets in most pubs, this one is on nearly all the
time. The publican and his wife admit they leave it on
mainly for their own amusement, but it remains on even when
they are too busy to pay attention.

The set has little effect on activities. The domino
playing pensioners can easily disregard it and do so almost
completely. Other patrons, both regulars and the few casual
visitors, watch mostly in the early evenings, when only a
handful are present, but even then conversation goes on. As
the pub fills normal bustle and talk muffle the audio, but
the volume is not turned up to compensate. The regulars,
nearly all men at first, splinter into smaller groups as
friends and wives come in, but the groups are generally

separated by sex, and they spread along the various tables
and at the end of the bar counter next to the door. The
darts board also gets much use. Only some regular loners and
occasional casual visitors ordinarily sit at the bar counter
close enough to the television to hear clearly, and they
frequently break their attention to talk with the hosts or
one another.

The television complements the longstanding use of the
pub. The regulars use the relatively crowded peak hours to
interact with their closest "mates." Television helps take up
the slack at other times. At peak hours the television, by
occupying loners and strangers at one end of the bar counter,
probably reduces their exchanges with the regulars, but this
is a very hospitable house, and these same people are readily
brought in at the less hectic times. The set never commands
attention; rather, to break into a program with unrelated
talk does not breach etiquette unless the program holds
exceptional appeal.

The replacement of a regulars' system by other uses and
features is more often the outcome of a gradual, multifaceted
process than of a singular and sudden environmental change.
The recent history of the Duke Charles "Public Bar" (Figure
17) provides a good example.

In spite of its moderately large size, quite a lot of
"cozy" space remains. Seating and tables are ample, and
together with some partial room dividers and other

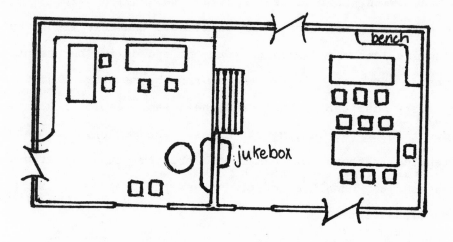

Figure 17. "Public Bar," the <u>Duke Charles</u>, Fenston

furnishings partly enclose spaces that vary enough in size to accomodate a variety of social groups. The design is socially versatile, in short. The division of the room into two parts, one raised three steps above the other and each provided with central service over a short bar counter, should allow a division of clientele and use, but what is instead happening is the replacement of the regulars' system by the youth system and classic public bar use.

The regulars still come in but no longer dominate the life of the room. They have stopped doing many of the things that regulars do, and do not interact as effectively throughout the pub, because so many competing activities are going on that involve a very different clientele. Their use is in sum more casual, more like that of a classic public bar. The Duke Charles has long received a sizeable number of casual visitors - situated near the main square, it is open through the afternoon on market days - but in recent years a young crowd has moved in. Though they have a reputation for being "rough," they do not seem to intimidate the regulars (at least not those who remain), but they are numerous and boisterous, tending to push the regulars into the periphery more by dominating the center stage than by anything else.

It is hard to sort through the many factors that have propelled the change, except that most are reducible to the deliberate policies of the publican. He has cultivated the young crowd, albeit not without rows with some of them, a

move that is profitable, since these patrons spend heavily on
drinks, but also something rooted in the publican's idea of
progress. He often refers to traditional pub activities as
old fashioned, is proud of extensive renovations, many of
them by his own labors, and is eager to show them to visiting
ethnographers or anyone else who expresses interest.

Darts and dominoes teams, a thrift club, and a sick club
were all dropped during the few years prior to the field
work, the teams, according to the landlord, because of
internecine bickering and the lack of anyone willing to take
the lead in organizing and managing them. A social club has
been started, and its membership is about equal to the old
clubs, fluctuating a bit between 40 and 50, mostly old
regulars. Once a year it sponsors an outing. This club
notwithstanding, organized participation in the pub is down.
The landlord states that interest in such things has fallen
off, but other publicans that also report difficulties
recruiting people to lead the sick and thrift clubs have kept
them going by taking over. The brewery that owns this pub
helps publicans do so by offering assistance with the books
and arranging interest on the principal.

The regulars come in less frequently today. They still
play cribbage and dominoes, but now sporadically, whereas
play was once almost constant, according to the publican and
several of the patrons. Perhaps most significantly, the
regulars do not bring their sons or daughters into the pub,

or meet them there. The young people who frequent this house
are unrelated to and for the most part little known to the
regulars outside of the pub.

The landlord has furnished this room with a staff of
young barmaids and a jukebox, to which the young patrons
respond by generating a high level of noise at peak hours.
The trade also peaks very sharply on weekends; on Friday and
Saturday evenings the bustle begins at opening time and never
lets up.

The regulars of the Duke Charles have lost too many of
their traditional functions at the core of the pub's social
life, and their activities are too much diluted and intruded
upon by other uses of the pub for the regulars' system to
maintain its vitality. Regulars of other pubs still use the
"Public Bar" quite a lot as a pint stop, but its role as a
local is dying. The young clientele makes it their pub, but
not their local in the well understood sense.

The Duke Charles is not unique in the decline of clubs
and teams. Sick and thrift clube have in Bolton and Fenston
declined slowly but steadily in number and membership.
Publicans' efforts to preserve them are generally successful,
but are being made less often than in a few past years.
Informants and brewers' representatives indicated the trend
is nationwide, though not universal. Most pubs long ago
dropped such excursions as pigeon races and trips to the
beach. The decline of the more organized activities

represents some decline of commitment of the regulars to the
local, and the staff of the local to the regulars, but while
the process in most leaves the regulars' system essentially
intact, at the Duke Charles the sum of those things that make
up the regulars' system has fallen below a critical point.

Returning to television and its effects, three Bolton
licensed rooms, the "Public Bars" of a house in the primary
sample and two in the secondary sample, were found in which a
set is left on constantly, in each with more drastic effect
than in the Royal Arms. Social interaction splinters among
groups of one to four persons, and many older patrons spend
long hours doing nothing but sipping beer and watching. All
three rooms are crowded at peak hours, but the volume is loud
enough to be audible throughout and capable of being followed
in much of the space. The presence of the set has a
remarkable dampening effect upon casual exchanges among the
patrons. Small tables and extra chairs have been added, some
even aligned for viewing the set, to accomodate the new use.
These observations seem to confirm the opinions of some
publicans and patrons at other Bolton pubs, where television
was present but little used; namely, constant use destroys
the social life.

SUMMARY

A system of human interaction with a built environment
like the pub inevitably generates traditional symbolic

associations, and at the same time draws identity and
integrity from those associations, but rigid conformity is
not required even if the system is long established. The end
of the regulars' system might be read in the worst fears of
critics of pub change; the last old regular will trade in his
grey overcoat for some trendy wraps, march into a lavender
scented great hall of a lounge holding hands with his wife,
and tell the waitress, "two vodka lime fizzes, luv, with ice
cream." In reality the regulars, while adaptable, are not so
pliable, and the brewers are in the aggregate more mindful of
tradition than their critics fear.

New systems do not yet have the same capacity to maintain
their identity, nor do they have defenders who would take the
brewers, magistrates, and publicans to task for their
perceived destruction. The youth system is fairly rich in
symbols, but many of these are drawn from a context far
broader than just pubs, and even those peculiar to the pubs
are not adhered to very strongly; the fashion for keg bitter
and some mixed drinks does not prevent most of the
participants drinking beer from the barrel. The growth of
open space at the expense of "cozy," the decline of some of
the regulars' functions, and the shift of pub entertainment
to forms that demand less of the patrons all signal the
growth of the newer systems at the expense of the old, but at
this time all of these trends appear to have definite limits.
The postwar boom in pub construction and renovation has

slowed.   Old patterns of pub use will continue to evolve;
whether at some point continuity is lost with present systems
probably depends on future directions within the whole
society.

THE PUB IN THE COMMUNITY

Pubs and pubgoers play their roles not in a vacuum but as parts of a larger community. The systems that have been described encompass the salient changes within pubs. It is now incumbent to place these changes in their wider social and cultural context.

First to be dealt with will be the pubs of Bolton and Fenston, how they fit into those communities, and who goes where and why. The remainder of the chapter is devoted to generalizing about trends in the whole nation: the control of pubs and marketing, the make up of the clientele, and the place of the pub as a community center.

FENSTON

Map 1 places the pubs of Fenston in their spatial context amid streets, neighborhoods, and important community features and services. It has been redrawn to disguise the town's identity, but the relation of pubs to places has been maintained as faithfully as possible. The town center is still central but the sectors radiating outward have been juxtaposed and some natural features altered.

Map 1.   Fenston pubs, November, 1970

Map 2 illustrates the elimination of pubs at various times during the last thirty years. In addition, dates are given for the years of housing estate additions, both private and public ("council").

The rate of license reduction is striking, from 42 in 1939 to 15 at the end of my field work in June, 1972. The whole district of which Fenston is a major part has had one of the highest pub to people ratios in England for as long as records have been kept. Despite the reductions Fenston retains a pub for about every 650 people, slightly better than the national average of roughly one to every 700 Englishmen. The eliminated houses have almost all been small pubs with only one licensed room in regular use, and have tended to be those away from the town center, except that the Gunner (#5) and the Union Jack (#6) have expanded to accommodate the trade from the adjacent housing estates.

Older informants agreed that the Fenston pubs were quite crowded in the years before World War II. How many of their remembrances are colored by nostalgia is difficult to say, but the trade of the houses must be presumed to have been great enough to support them, greater than that of the smallest houses today. Most informants agreed that a considerable falling off of trade occurred in the years immediately following the war. The greatest mumber of licenses were eliminated during the 1950's.

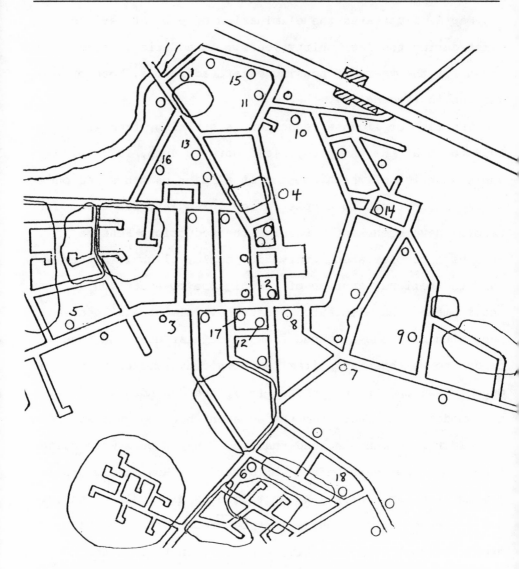

Key: Numbered pubs were licensed in November, 1970.

Unnumbered circles were licenses eliminated 1939-70.

Housing estates and years of completion are encircled.

Map 2.   Reduction of Fenston Licenses, 1939-1970

As a whole then, Fenston exhibits the decline of small, cozy neighborhood pubs that is evident throughout the nation. These are far from extinct, however, and some of Fenston's "locals" show signs of carrying on for some time to come. The present pubs of Fenston can be arrayed along a spectrum, from what might be termed the coziest to the opposite, a large pub consisting of two sprawling lounges.

The former, the Leg of Lamb (#17), consists, for all intents and purposes, of a single room. The landlady's sitting room is also licensed but used on few occasions. The main licensed room is shown in Figure 18.

Note the lack of a bar counter; drinks are brought in from the kitchen directly behind the door on the right hand side of the figure. This pub has an exceptionally steady clientele, at my best estimate about 35 regulars, including a half dozen women. In addition, a number of the regulars' wives come in occasionally, but do not take enough part to be called regulars. Casual visitors are few and newcomers seldom repeat. All the younger male patrons have fathers who are regulars. Interestingly, this is quite a hospitable house, and it should not be thought that newcomers are driven away. For instance, I was readily adopted into the regular clique. But the pub is so cozy as to make some visitors express discomfort, and sufficiently lacking in modern chic to seem prosaic to others: "I went in there once and the landlord had never heard of a bloody Bacardi."

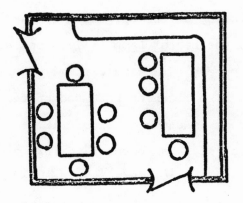

Figure 18. Serving Room, the <u>Leg</u> <u>of</u> <u>Lamb</u>, Fenston

The entire pub then is an archetypical regulars' citadel, spoken of by both its own patrons and those at other pubs as more a club than a pub. When relatively empty (up to about a half dozen persons), men and women converse from all corners of the room. The landlord and his wife join in, all the while going back and forth for drinks, mostly beer. An order is seldom necessary, only an empty glass and a nod of the head.

As the pub fills, Sunday afternoons and after nine o'clock most evenings, some men break off to play dominoes, often with the landlord joining them. Others, mostly the women, talk at the table near the door or among the nearby benches, but no patrons are out of touch with the rest.

At the opposite extreme from the Leg of Lamb is the Frigate, a pub on the river (#1) and long ago furnished with an interior modeled on a sailing ship theme. Both main rooms, a "Lounge Bar" and a "Public Bar" named in line with the prices charged, are lounges in every sense, and they are laid out as the two legs of an 'L' around a central service area. Off the "Public Bar" is an additional seating area with no separate bar counter service. The bar counter in each of the main lounges runs nearly the length of the room and comprises the whole of the service.

The seating capacity is close to 50 persons in both rooms, about 15 in a side room. The "Lounge Bar" is seldom filled to capacity. It draws a rather irregular trade,

except at weekday noon hours when it draws a small but fairly
dependable luncheon trade, mostly from local businessmen.
The clientele of this room is almost entirely middle aged,
while the "Public Bar" is dominated by a young trade, the
majority of whom are single. The young frequently fill their
room, but only quite late. After ten o'clock on weekend
evenings, a crowd of 30 or so mills around in front of the
bar counter, along with many more at the tables.

No other Fenston pubs are on the same scale as the
Frigate, but three others can be placed in the next class:
the Lion Hotel (#2, see Figure 10, Chapter Five), the Duke
Charles (#4, see Figure 17, Chapter Five), and the Black
Stallion (#3). Lounge setttings dominate all three. Other
pubs with only one room in regular use include numbers 9
through 16, although 9 and 10 are a bit larger than the
others and do a larger volume of trade. Service in the one
room pubs is across a short bar counter, and the room plan is
decidedly sociopetal. The middle range of pubs, numbers 5
through 8, are intermediate in both their size and design,
Most have an open lounge plus a regulars' citadel, either a
small, cozy room or an area somehow set apart to one side of
an additional room on the lounge pattern. One example is the
Union Jack (#6), described and illustrated in Chapter Five.

Looking at the current map of Fenston, most residential
areas are convenient to more than one type of pub, though the
larger pubs, apart from the Frigate, are concentrated in the

center. In investigating the geography of pubgoing in
Fenston, it seemed desirable to establish both the habits of
the regulars, i.e., the distribution of their locals, and the
pattern of casual visiting. For a time, a door to door
survey was considered, aimed at mapping the effect of home
location on pub choice, but most of this information turned
out to be more reliably obtained at the other end, by working
in the pubs (Appendix Two).

The first step was to estimate the numbers of male
regulars. A figure of between seven and nine hundred was
arrived at, a minimum, since it was calculated by counting
the number of people in the regulars' roles in each pub
during the period of observation. A range is given because
of some discrepancy between observational findings and
questionnaire data. Respondents were first counted as
regulars who described themselves that way and said either
that they visited one pub at least once a week or belonged to
a pub team or club. Just under 700 met these criteria. From
observation it appeared that some respondents came in less
often than they recalled, but a greater number did so more
often, and in other less precisely definable ways appeared to
be regulars, yet failed to describe themselves as such, not
too surprisingly, since the term is not used popularly with
complete consistency.

The minimum number of women who are regulars was
estimated in like manner at about two hundred, give or take a

dozen or two. This includes women at pubs where they are
highly integrated with the male regulars and those in which
the sexes carry on separately much of the time.

In general, the local turns out to be within a half mile
of the regular's house. Except in those neighborhoods in
which only one pub is convenient, the local was less often
the very nearest than one a bit more distant. Older patrons
(over 60 for the most part) tend to go further afield for
their local than the younger ones, not necessarily because
they are more fit, but because they do not wander to other
pubs to nearly the same extent, and they tend to remain in
their local most of the afternoon or evening.

Given their concentration on one pub, the older regulars
quite naturally tend to be more particular about their choice
of local. Much more frequently than others they stress the
beer (both the brand and other factors) and specific
conveniences as reasons for choosing a particular local.
They also favor pubs in which they have known the publican
for some time, not too difficult in several of the smaller
houses that have landlords over 60 years of age. The
dramatic reduction in the number of licenses within their
lifetimes has often forced older patrons to wander some
distance to find a local that meets their preferences. Many
reported that after their local of many years closed down
they tried to find a substitute as much like the original as
possible. The youngest pubgoers are either much more vague

why they choose a particular pub, or they have a reason which
is quite different from those of the older pubgoers, e.g., a
lot of young women go there.

Married women regulars mainly attend the same local as
their husbands. Younger women may travel further, especially
if their usual haunt is the site of a thriving youth system.
As a case in point, several single women travel several
nights a week to the Lion Hotel "Lounge Bar" from a town
eight miles away.

Men tend to visit one small house in addition to their
local (whatever its size) and to wander the larger pubs in
the center of town. Women tend more to pair two favorite
pubs and do not in general travel far if they must walk.
Some go to one pub frequently with their husbands, and
occasionally to another with a woman friend or relative.

The effect of growing car ownership has been felt in
recent years. The most immediate influence on the owners'
pubgoing habits is to increase the range of casual visits.
Regulars remain faithful to their local when they acquire a
car. Those who travel some distance to their local were
found to have moved from the neighborhood, or their old local
had closed.

Older patrons do not ordinarily change their arrangements
for meeting people when they acquire a car; they continue to
go to the pubs alone except when a team match or other
special occasion necessitates a mass move from one pub to

another. Young people, however, often meet at a local or
cafe and then ride in groups to distant houses. They also
range more widely on average than the older pubgoers. Quite
a few drive often to neighboring towns and cities, something
one group of older single men also did several nights a week.

BOLTON

In Bolton exact statistics regarding pubs and lists of
former licenses were not forthcoming from the licensing
authorities, but enough data were available from canvassing
and from other municipal officials, brewery representatives,
and neighborhood informants to reveal the trends in pub
numbers and distribution. Bolton had 304 pubs in 1937 (Mass-
Observation 1970:67), 180 when the field work began. Houses
have long been concentrated in the town center and along the
main roads radiating out toward neighboring communities, and
the steady elimination of pubs from back streets has
accentuated the pattern. Reduction has been due in part to
the fact that many of these were small houses that have
become uneconomical to operate, but also due to the
liquidation of licenses in neighborhoods being torn down for
urban renewal. In addition, the rapid falling off of noon
and after work business around the mills has spelled the end
of many.

Two older neighborhoods retain a higher density of back
street pubs than the rest of the town. These, however, are

slated for clearance, and the housing estates which will
replace them will have a smaller number of pubs, and those
pubs will be large.

Consolidation was actually well under way in the 1930's,
and the pace did not measurably pick up during the immediate
postwar years. During the 1960's, however, Bolton became a
scene of rapid rebuilding and renovation in the pubs.

Before World War II new public housing estates included
no new pubs, but main roads were usually close enough to give
inhabitants access to several houses. Current policy
provides one or two for each estate, very large in size and
with all rooms, regardless of nomenclature, built on a lounge
pattern. The policy of licensing authorities, city planners,
and brewers is that licenses should ordinarily be issued only
if parking is ample. Catering is also encouraged.

Like those of Fenston, the pubs of Bolton form a spectrum
according to size, but they cannot be so easily lumped into
distinct categories in which size, layout and social use
converge. The Mass-Observation team used a three part
classification: small, medium and large, but the criteria are
not specific. The small pubs then tended to have beer (only)
licenses, a rarity today. The average Bolton pubs is
considerably larger than that of Fenston; even the remaining
back street houses typically have two or three times the
floor space of their Fenston counterparts, with longer bar
counters and a larger volume of trade.

Before World War II the majority of the Bolton pubs were laid out according to the "hall plan," with a hall and best rooms placed behind the service area of the public bar. The largest examples of the type survive. Those in the town center tended to have large lounges on the "best" side even before the war, while those on the outer roads were large by virtue of a proliferation of small rooms off the hall.

Bolton informants were as certain as those of Fenston that all pubs did a thriving trade in the prewar years, though the number of neighborhood houses eliminated in the 1930's for lack of trade was quite high. Judging from the descriptions and counts in The Pub and the People, the smaller locals were full mainly at peak weekend hours, but most neighborhood pubs had enough regulars any evening to form several distinct groups.

Groups of wandering male pubgoers are more a feature of the Bolton landscape than Fenston's. For the most part, the "mates" stay within their own neighborhood, though they vary their routes as they spread out from the local, especially where two main roads or the town center are within walking distance. Particular pubs are often shunned by individuals or groups because of a past fight with the publican, a dislike for the beer, or for some less tangible reason, but otherwise the pubs of the neighborhood will all be visited on a fairly regular basis. The Bolton wanderers in general visit a wider variety of houses than is the case in Fenston.

Most of the pubs on the groups' rounds are within a mile or a mile and a half of the local, a range that provides a great deal of variety if one begins near the town center or in some of the older neighborhoods.

Some individuals wander farther afield, even on foot or by bus. Bus service is sparse at closing time, often necessitating a walk back after going out by bus. Bolton pubgoers as a whole are more willing to walk long distances than those of Fenston, and young singles are especially likely to travel two and three miles, usually to pubs in the center of town. Older pubgoers mostly travel this far only for special events, such as interpub darts matches. The use of automobiles for pubgoing is much the same as in Fenston. Groups of young singles, mixed or of one sex, meet in pubs or other places and go to distant pubs, and a few groups of married men in their late twenties and early thirties also motor together. Older married men and couples drive to pubs if they have cars, but do not generally ferry their "mates" about to various houses. Several men with cars expressed the opinion that driving friends around is risky because of the risk of arrest for drunken driving.

A number of cozy settings are available in all the older neighborhoods of Bolton, even those near the town center, but they account for only a small part of the total trade. In small houses most of the trade consists of regulars. Today, the local for most regulars is a pub like about three-fifths

of those in Bolton. It includes a large lounge and a "Public
Bar" of varying size but always smaller than the lounge. In
the newer houses the "Public Bar" is laid out on a lounge
pattern. It must be concluded that a large proportion of the
regulars do not require a cozy citadel for their activities.
In this sense Bolton's regulars are less traditionally minded
than those of Fenston. Realizing the range of choices
available in at least the older neighborhoods, the fact that
pubs on the newer model do serve as locals, while nearby
older style houses remain only partly filled, indicates that
the pattern of renovation can to a degree be viewed as a
response to public demand.

But the public has also been prompted. Renovation along
modern lines came early to Bolton and has been actively
promoted ever since. Choice of pubs involves more than just
picking one by size and design type; the reasons may be quite
personal. What does one do when his local is totally
reconstructed? At Bolton pubs whose layout has been altered
within the last few years (including two in the primary
sample), the bulk of the present regulars date from before
the changes were made, yet most were nostalgic about the old
surroundings. It is fair to assume that these feelings are
genuine but not strong enough to override old loyalties. The
contrast with Fenston is meaningful. Fenston's regulars have
found their locals torn down, not rebuilt. The two
exceptions, the Union Jack and the Gunner, were reconstructed

so as to leave suitable space for regulars' citadels. As was
mentioned, displaced regulars sought out new locals closely
resembling the old.

Simply having a cozy pub available may be meaningless to
an old regular if his choices have been reduced. Nostalgia is
rarely expressed as a longing for one pub, but usually as a
statement that the pubs "around here" are no longer what they
used to be. Bolton pubgoers may simply be recognizing that
their pubs on the whole have changed and that to seek out
traditional style pubs, as in Fenston, would be futile.

In Bolton pubs of the primary sample it was found that
many sons had followed their fathers into the local. Thus,
the existing small pubs and regulars' rooms can be expected
to carry on their traditional functions for some time.
Current use of "bar in hall" design in many main road pubs
could facilitate this even though these houses are very
crowded at peak hours. Most of the remaining small locals do
a fair volume of trade, and the brewers have no plans to
eliminate them, but outside intervention could bring about
their elimination. Urban renewal has removed many
neighborhood houses, and dooms many more, including one for
certain in the primary sample.

SUPPLY, DEMAND AND POLICY

License reduction in Fenston has lagged behind the
decline of trade. In Bolton urban renewal and the vigor of

renovation have reduced choice and to some degree preceded
change in pubgoing habits. We might well ask which community
is the more repesentative of nationwide trends.

In comparing prewar Bolton with Fulham, in southwest
London, Mass-Observation concludes "it would therefore seem
as if compulsory inhibiting of drink-opportunity does keep
down the number who drink in pubs..." [1970:110]. Studies of
the vast housing estates and new towns lead to the same
conclusion, since these areas invariably have a low pub
density and also reduced attendance. Choice is also
typically restricted to large houses with rooms built almost
entirely upon lounge patterns. Residents find the supply of
pubs a fait accompli and no doubt have their habits molded by
convenience.

Cauter and Downham (1954) drew a sample of Derby
households, and conducted interviews focusing on
participation and attendance in public and domestic events.
The pubs trail the cinema, churches and theaters in the
number of people who ever attend, but pubs attract the
highest percentage of "keen participants," about a third of
the total adult population (1954:201). About three quarters
of the adult men and one third of the adult women at least
occasionally attend pubs. About one third of the pubgoers
take part in darts, dominoes, cards, and snooker or
billiards. Fifty-two percent of those people who go to pubs
once a week or more often engage in these social activities.

The pub is a meeting place, but falls short of being the neighborhood nerve center that is sometimes portrayed, say, in the popular televison series, Coronation Street; in its pubs a closely knit neighborhood passes gossip and resolves problems and conflicts. In reality 40% of English adults never set foot in pubs (Cooper, 1970), and regular patrons are presumably much fewer. Decision-making and conflict resolution could hardly be normal pub functions, when pub conversation is so dominated by sports and inconsequential talk.

Pubs are quiet in most rural communities or are dominated by motorists from a distance. This practice has increased in recent years; brewery representatives maintained that cars have revitalized the country pub. Yet pubs were once vital centers of village life.

> Village inns and taverns have existed for centuries,
> and were, until quite recently, the only places where
> controversial subjects such as religion, trade-union
> activities, or politics, could be freely discussed.
> Fifty years ago, they were, much more than today,
> village social clubs, popular with the men who could be
> found there most evenings in the week discussing a
> great variety of national and local subjects which
> interested or concerned them (Bracey 1959:153).

The contrast with the present pubs of towns and cities could not be more evident, both in the degree of participation and in the content of communication. My study of rural houses was not intensive, but the absence of anything remotely like what Bracey describes is so apparent that it is hard to imagine many fulfilling these functions,

the same conclusion reached by Bracey. Exceptions are to be
found, however, places where the pub is still a focus of the
community. In W.W. Williams' (1963) study of a West Country
village, "Ashworthy," the minority that is not Noncomformist
in religion uses the pub in ways reminiscent of Bracey's
description.

Real communities have means of dealing with conflict, but
in most pubs the mechanisms of resolving conflict among them
are weak, hence it is simply avoided. If a pub were a
community center in the broadest sense, the social contacts
among its patrons would be replicated elsewhere, but instead
the relationships of the typical pub "mates" are usually
restricted to that context.

The pub is thus not a community center in most places,
not a link binding the pubgoer to the total social fabric.
One large part of any community never visits, while another
seeks only amusement, perhaps choosing at the last moment
between pub and cinema. The significant minority that has a
defined role in the pub, the regulars and some participants
in the youth and businessmen's lunch systems, take part in a
subculture of sorts, but one that is typically both more
specialized and more isolated than in former times.

CLASS AND THE PUBS

Cauter and Downham (1954:96) found that about the same
percentage of working class and middle class adults in Derby

visit pubs at least occasionally, 53% and 54%, respectively,

but 34% of the working class visit pubs once a week or more,

compared with only 21% of the middle class. Most

commentators and informants agree that the pubs gained full

middle class repectability during World War II, but

unfortunately no prewar comparative figures are available for

Derby or anywhere else. Some of the middle class always went

to pubs, and pub disreputability varied from place to place;

in a few prewar Lancashire towns, mill owners drank with

their workers at the noon hour, while in most other places

they were more apt to go to "gentlemen's rooms."

The postwar era ended class segregation, and today a

middle class clientele rarely predominates to the near

exclusion of others, other than in hotels and other

establishments catering to travelers and tourists. More pubs

are distinctly working class, owing to their being buried

deep within those neighborhoods, yet even these see the

exceptional middle class patron; students in particular make

a point of seeking out rustic pubs in old working class

neighborhoods.

While no social regulations today maintain middle class

or working class pubs, class differences are still manifest

in pubgoing habits. Different proportions of clientele in

certain types of pubs reflect class preferences. The most

obvious difference is a middle class preference for certain

archaic architectural styles, in particular Tudor, and to a

lesser extent Georgian. Pubs in these styles tend to contain
a decidedly larger percentage of middle class customers than
otherwise comparable houses built in other styles.

Bolton has several pubs in archaic styles. One was in
the primary sample, and a special effort was made there and
in three other houses to ascertain the occupations of a
significant part of the clientele. Three of the pubs,
including the one in the primary sample, are on the periphery
of town, on streets within predominantly working class
residential areas but near private housing estates which
contain a very high number of nonmanual workers. All three
houses attract a socially diverse clientele including many
middle class people. Nearby pubs, all of comparatively
nondescript early twentieth century styles, retain an almost
entirely working class trade. In the center of town, one
genuinely old Tudor pub draws a large businessmen's lunch
trade in spite of competition with hotel bars better set up
for meals. At night this same pub attracts a young crowd,
mostly advanced students, apprentice businessmen and young
professionals.

Three of the four brewery representatives interviewed,
though reluctant to state any strong class differences in
modern pubgoing habits, were of the opinion that
accessability to middle class residential areas is a strong
argument for maintaining a period appearance. To do so can
be costly, owing to the costs of horse brasses and other

paraphernalia. The fourth representative disagreed strongly, asserting that class no longer has any meaning with respect to pub choice, in fact that the concept of class is dead in England. All agreed that country pubs in Tudor style became extremely popular near suburban areas once car ownership became widespread.

A bonafide claim by virtue of age to the archaic style appears to help in attracting an established middle class patronage. "Pseudo-Tudor" and other plastic facsimiles of old styles are associated more with pubs that draw a young crowd.

> Broadly speaking, your working man living in, say, North or South London or the East End, will expect a lively house preferably with music, and an evening that finishes with a crescendo of noise, laughter, breaking glass and shouts of 'last orders!' But your middle class Londoner, once rowdy student days are behind him - students are the bane of London pubs - will like a fairly quiet, decently-run place, with a bit of history, where he can sit and talk, without back-ground noise, live or taped (Green and White 1968:13).

The implied ideology holds the key to class stylistic preferences. The renewed respectability of middle class pubgoing has brought into the pubs many people whose contact with them used to be slight. Others, those who have grown up with pubs as an integral part of their lives, have too many ingrained social considerations involved in their pub choices to pay too much heed to "a bit of history."

That is not to say that only the neophytes take note of archaic styles. Informants of all ages and social classes repeatedly cited pubs in Tudor style when asked about

"typical" pubs, and the same style is projected in the media
and in fairs and exhibitions abroad as somehow representative
of The English Pub. Yet even by a liberal estimate, less
than five percent of English pubs could possibly fit this
description. Quite aside from the often postulated national
bent for nostalgia, it seems legitimate to say that the style
is identified with the true and genuine in pubs to a degree
that is out of all proportion to its real importance.

Geographical mobility, more than the direct effect of
income or occupation, accounts for the observed class
differences in pub choice. In Fenston and Bolton a long
established and mostly locally born segment of the middle
class participates as regulars at many predominantly working
class neighborhood pubs. Shopkeepers and other small
businessmen are especially in evidence, people with strong
everyday community ties. It is relevant here to note certain
communities in which far more pubs than usual are built in
archaic styles: (1) historic towns and villages in which all
buildings are required to follow a period tradition, (2)
Oxford and Cambridge, and (3) resort towns in areas such as
the Lakes Country and the Derbyshire hills. The two
university towns and the resort centers have in common a
large number of middle class people with no lifetime roots.
The archaic pub styles have universal sentimental appeal, but
acting on these sentiments is left to those who have no ties
to the local pubs.

Green and White's allusion to "fairly quiet, well-run
places" also best applies to the mobile business and
professional classes, quite logically, since in the absence
of long standing ties within the pubs they visit, the bistro
system would be the use that would suit them best. Tudor
pubs also tend to be such places, and some specifically
middle class uses of pubs, notably entertaining business
clients, would perhaps be out of place in really boisterous
pubs.

Many symbolic aspects of class behavior in pubs have lost
their meaning. One of the most important changes has been in
the beverages consumed.

> Friday, May 7 [1938], a smallish pub in Higher Bridge
> Street, mid-day, two working class men of about 30 come
> into the vault and order small ports. This causes a
> profound sensation, the landlord literally taking a
> step backward, and repeating in an incredulous loud
> voice "small ports" [Mass-Observation 1970:47].

This reaction would be extremely improbable today. The
old associations of mild ale with working class men, cheap
port and stout with their wives and girlfriends, and better
port and sherry with middle class quaffers are all but gone,
and working class affluence is no doubt a major reason.
Bitter has replaced mild as the standard draught beer as the
price differential has become inconsequential to most
pubgoers. I do not mean to imply that no tendencies for
drink preferences by class persist - field work suggested
several - but the great majority of drinks consumed by all

pubgoers are drunk by blue collar and white collar patrons
alike, if not always in the same proportion.

AGE AND PUBGOING

   One theme of popular and scholarly literature is that
young married men today are more home oriented than their
fathers, and spend time and money there that used to go to
the pubs. If correct one would expect a significant effect
on the age distribution of pubgoers. In Fenston the data
fitted the generalization, patrons being predominantly at the
extremes of the legal age range. On weekend nights nearly
half the clientele are young, mainly under 25 and single. A
majority of several nights a week customers are over 50, and
a smaller number of the youth go that often, mostly to the
Lion Hotel "Lounge Bar" and the "Public Bar" of The Duke
Charles. Bolton, in contrast, was more in line with the
breakdown in Derby in the early 1950's (Table II). Bolton's
regulars were more evenly distributed by age than Fenston's,
whether the pubs were large or small, town center or
neighborhood.

   "Gimmick" pubs, built on a theme, are intended to
attract young patrons, the more extreme examples exclusively
so. The most flamboyant I found was a pub near Manchester in
which each room is extravagantly coordinated to its own

Table II

Pubgoing in Derby, by Age Categories

Age interval	Frequency of pub visits (in % of that interval)				
	Daily	>1/week	1/week	<1/week	Never
18-24	-	11	12	22	55
25-34	2	19	20	24	35
35-44	4	13	13	27	43
45-54	5	12	12	25	46
55-69	6	12	8	17	57

Source: Cauter and Downham (1954).

theme. One room, on a South Seas motif, has a pool in the
center with live "alligators," actually caimans. The crowd
here is almost entirely young and single.

SUMMARY

Pub changes hint at shifts in social use, but
generalization should allow for the flexibility of the
pubgoing public. The increasing respectability of middle
class pubgoing favors the development of the bistro system.
Middle class people with strong local roots were in the past
little inhibited by the mores regarding pubs, and continue
like the bulk of the working class to make multiple use of
them. The geographically mobile middle class people most
readily fit into the less socially integrated bistro system.
Lounge use is increasing among all classes and ages, but
lounge use is itself diverse. Young people go to the pubs
more today. The youth system makes use of space in much the
same way as the bistro system, and thus a graduation of young
pubgoers into a pattern of lounge visiting with spouses can
be envisioned as the new life cycle for pubgoers. But many
of these same young people take over or inherit ties to a
local as well. Multiple use of pubs can be expected to
continue among those segments of the population that have an
active tradition of pubgoing.

Economic factors favor central service and large rooms
in pubs, yet these need not constrain use within rigid

bounds. Social legislation through design is the legacy of

the "improved public house" movement. It is possible instead

to direct ingenuity toward evolving flexible designs that

meet economic needs and also permit varied use.

THE PUB AND ENGLISH SOCIAL CHANGE

Pub change has a direct bearing on two very prominent debates in the sociological literature on current English social trends. One controversial thesis is that the classes are converging, another that a mass, media-dominated society is emerging. The pub fits into both debates, the first because it is an important traditional working class institution, and the second because it is a place for socializing that has lost many of its functions as a center for communication.

CLASS CHANGE

The Traditional Working Class

In the mid-1950's some researchers from the Institute of Community Studies (London) began a study of Bethnal Green, an old working class district of East London. In accord with the literature on modern, industrial societies they expected to find that the nuclear family dominates kin relations, while larger networks of kin have comparatively few functions. "Thus prepared, we were surprised to discover that the wider family, far from having disappeared, was still very much alive in the middle of London" (Young and Willmott 1957:32).

Their discoveries were that kinship ties have important mutual assistance functions, are the source of most social contacts within the home, mold the pattern of neighborhood contacts, and have a strong effect upon residence patterns. At the heart of the system is "mum;" home is spoken of as "me mum's." Men and women who have married and left their parents' homes visit frequently, but the women significantly more often. Both see their mothers somewhat more often than their fathers. Informants emphasized the bond between mother and daughter in a number of ways, both practical and sentimental.

> The mother is the head and center of the extended
> family, her home its meeting place. 'Mum's' is the
> family rendezvous,' as one wife said. Her daughters
> congregate at the mother's, visiting her more often
> than she visits any of them: 68% of married women last
> saw their mother at her home, and only 27% at their
> own. When there, they quite often see their other
> sisters, and brothers too, particularly if they are
> still living at home, and even if they live elsewhere,
> the sisters may call there at the usual time in the
> afternoon for a cup of tea, or just happen to drop in
> for a chat on their way to the shops. Regular weekly
> meetings often supplement the day-to-day visiting
> (Young and Willmott 1957:32).

Bethnal Green neighbors rarely visit one another in their homes. The ideal neighbor is there to provide assistance in emergencies and shares a feeling of neighborhood solidarity, but in all ordinary times "keeps himself to himself."

Postmarital residence tends strongly to be matrilocal. Residence near the wife's "mum" is a much preferred state of affairs, a preference that many couples realize even in the face of a chronic housing shortage. As a rule newlyweds

prefer their own apartment, but if income or other factors
force them to move in with parents, they most often go to the
young wife's home.

What emerges from the report is the strength of a network
of mothers and daughters, its functions centered on the home.
The rearing of children, the furnishing of the home, and
other domestic concerns are by custom the responsibility of
the woman, who draws a great deal on her mother for guidance.

Corroboration of the Bethnal Green findings comes from a
number of sources, indicating that the salient features are
to be found in other established urban working class
communities in England. Parallels in "Ship Street,"
Liverpool (Kerr, 1957) include the importance of the mother-
daughter tie within a larger network of kin. In Barton Hall,
Bristol, Jennings found that "in terms of time spent together
the tie between mothers and daughters appeared to be most
close [of ties among relatives]" (1962:54). Also in Bethnal
Green, Bott (1958) called attention to the mother-daughter
link.

Matrilocality is documented in "Ship Street," a Yorkshire
coal mining town (Dennis, Henriques and Slaughter 1956:204-
205), and St. Ebbe's, Oxford (Mogey 1956). In a nationwide
survey of The People readers Gorer found "a marked tendency
toward matrilocality in the English working class" (1955:45).
Dennis et al and Kerr also found a preponderance of visits of

daughters to their mothers among all social contacts within the home.

To describe the group that centers on "mum", Firth and students and associates (Firth 1956) coined "matri-centered family," based on a study of "South Borough" in London during the mid-1950's. This is a similar community to those in the studies mentioned above, one in which similar conclusions were reached and the extended ties examined in somewhat greater detail.

This matri-centered family is sited in the home and dominates that place. The wife lives near her mother, sees her frequently and follows her lead in home making. Kerr (1958), Young and Willmott (1957), and Firth (1956) all report that "mum" is the essential link between sisters; it is in her home that they most often see one another. Contacts among cousins are to some degree dependent on their common maternal grandmother. On the death of their mother, sisters often drift apart, with the expected effect upon their daughters.

Where does all this leave the male? If the home is a female realm, then the existence of a masculine complement would provide a neat balance within the society. To a degree this complement is realized in work, club and betting shop, but one must be wary of cultural stereotypes that lead to exaggeration. Many sons follow their fathers into such occupations as dock-worker and become regulars in the same

pub or members of the same clus, but the bonds of recruitment
are generally far looser than those which tie together the
women of the matri-centered family. The symbols of the
female-male division are rich and abundant in the respective
settings - soft colors versus blacks and browns, flower
prints versus leather and stained wood - but these
associations are not intrinsic, after all, but have grown up
with the settings.

The stereotype of the English working man as one who
spends all his free time in the pubs is easily dismissed.
Its closest approximation in the sociological literature is
reported among the miners of "Ashton:"

> A man's centers of activity are outside his home; it is
> outside his home that there are located the criteria of
> success and social acceptance. He works and plays, and
> makes contacts with other men and women, outside his
> home. The comedian who defined 'home' as "the place
> where you fill the pools in on Wednesday night" was
> something of a sociologist. With the exception of a
> small minority of men who spend a good deal of time
> pottering about with household improvements or are
> passionately interested in some hobby, or are very
> newly married, the husbands of Ashton for preference
> come home for a meal after finishing work and as soon
> as they can feel clean and rested they look for the
> company of their mates, i.e. their friends of the same
> sex (Dennis, Henriques and Slaughter 1956:180-181).

Ashton men spend nearly every evening in the pubs, a
rarity judging from nationwide statistics on pubgoing or my
own observations. Ashton is unusual for its sharp division
of labor too. Few of the town's women are employed outside
the home. The authors feel that the demands of coal mining
reinforce the male ethic. In many ways then, Ashton

demonstrates the division of sex roles in exaggerated form, an extreme that demonstrates that sex roles and accompanying social behavior are flexible and responsive to altered circumstances.

Klein (1965) reviews the literature and concludes that the division of labor within the home, the exclusiveness of the male domain, and the distant, authoritative role of the father in the home are more marked in the North. The generalization fits popular conceptions, but the coverage of the nation thus far by detailed and relevant community studies has not been comprehensive.

Affluent Workers, New Communities, and Embourgeoisement

In England, as in the rest of the advanced capitalist world, a growing opinion is that the distinction between working class and middle class is becoming blurred, so much so that the whole class concept is obsolete. Surveys in which respondents are asked to name their social class find increasing numbers who demur, insisting that only snobs speak of class. Some journalists aver that class has no more meaning in England. It is apparent that English class distinctions do not have the same impact as they once did; the days are over when men entered the boss's office cap in hand, or when routine references were made to "betters" and "lower orders." Yet during the postwar years, when class was purportedly fading, Great Britain stood the lowest among

advanced western nations in social mobility by occupation
(Svalastoga 1959), and some sociological studies call
attention to persisting differences between the classes in
cultural behavior.

One reputed and plausible cause of class convergence is
the convergence of the earnings of clerical workers and the
better paid manual workers, which now overlap appreciably.
The overall income differential decreased during the early
1950's at a rather dramatic rate. On the other side, Titmuss
(1966) finds evidence of a more recent reversal of the trend,
and some writers, notably Coates and Silburn (1970), call
attention to sectors that have been left out of general
affluence, living in pockets of poverty.

A frequent corollary to the class convergence argument
makes cultural convergence a product of general affluence.
In this scenario the mode of life of the affluent workers,
their social organization, their material trappings, and
their values are becoming much like those sectors of the
established middle class whose incomes they now realize.

Much of the pertinenet research focuses on attitudes
toward work, on perceived models of society, and on political
alignments. One relevant theme is change in the major
patterns of family orientation.

Mention was made in the previous chapter of the theme of
the domestication of the working man, and some signs of the
phenomenon hinted at in Bolton and Fenston. A home centered

style of life involving both husband and wife reputedly approximates middle class life styles. Much of the debate on convergence focuses on the significance and extent of the change in home life.

Council estates have often been test cases, and a large body of evidence indicates that the observed changes have gone furthest and fastest in those places. The design of the homes, the plan of the estate, and the provision of amenities follow a middle class suburban model, albeit often in more austere fashion. The provision of a large front room and a kitchen too small to serve more than its utilitarian function are recurrent features that are contrary to traditional working class use of space. In the larger new towns, at least, the occupants have moved some distance from their old communities and close friends. Many take up commuting to work.

A number of studies of new towns and large council estates in the early stages of their development have found that men spend a great deal of time in the home. The garden replaces that now distant pub as the foremost place to spend leisure time. Working men's clubs seldom establish a good foothold. For all people, the woman especially, the importance of kinship is weakened by distance. This is not to imply that kinship ties lose their meaning to the people involved. Rather, the change is expressed in the drastically reduced number of social visits among kin and in such matters

as mutual aid and the giving of advice. Simultaneously,
status competition and other frictions arise among neighbors
(Young and Willmott, 1957; Jennings, 1962; Kuper, 1953;
Mogey, 1956).

Jennings (1962) and Mogey (1956) found an explicit
identification with the working class in older established
communities, but not in new estates. Klein (1965) was moved
to conclude that the inhabitants of the estates progress from
"status-assent" to "status-dissent," ending up by denying
class distinctions or by placing themselves high on the
status scale. Young and Willmott (1962) found a like pattern
of home centered social life, weakened extended family ties,
and increased status competion among working class people
moving into a suburban, previously mostly middle class town
in Essex.

The estates studied have been large, housing thousands.
In depth comparative study of a town like Fenston, where the
new estates are similarly planned but are too small to
effectively isolate the residents, might be of great value; I
found that moving to the estates had little effect on
pubgoing habits.

Using selected factories for a sample, Zweig (1952, 1961)
compared industrial workers of 1948 and 1958 and found that
even among those not living in the new estates, new attitudes
toward the home are emerging together with views of society
approximating to Klein's status dissent. Zweig and Klein

both conclude that convergence is in fact the adoption of a middle class way of life by the working class.

The sum of these shifts in the working class toward middle class patterns is termed the "embourgeoisement" thesis by Lockwood (1966) and Goldthorpe, Lockwood, Bechofer and Platt (1969), who counter that what is emerging is not so much a blue collar class with middle class culture, but instead a new type of person recognized in Lockwood's term, the "privatised worker." They reject the allegations of a decreasing gap between the manual and white collar occupations in their working conditions, satisfactions, and rewards. Of more direct relevance to the present study is the authors' assertion that the "new" workers view work instrumentally, i.e., are willing to accept an otherwise unrewarding job that pays well in order to afford the demands of a home. This is contrasted to middle class workers, whose status system reputedly molds the view that a job is a means of acquiring status. There is also an obvious contrast with the role of work in certain older communities like "Ashton" (Dennis et al 1956), where work is thoroughly integrated with a male ethic.

The workers interviewed by Goldthorpe, Lockwood, Bechofer and Platt all worked at four factories in Luton, chosen as a critical case, in part because it is a new town and in part because the four factories involved, employing a significant portion of the town's work force, pay unusually high wages.

In one the working conditions were affected by advanced

technology and allegedly exemplified what "embourgeoisement"

advocates have held would favor "the breakdown of traditional

antagonisms [between manual workers and management] within

the enterprise and the existence of a high level of normative

consensus" (Goldthorpe et al 1969:40).

The authors go on to stress the importance of changing

patterns of leisure and home life in the whole

embourgeoisement argument:

> Despite the attention given by certain writers to the
> impact on the working class of developments in the
> forces and relationships of production, the claim that
> the manual worker is being progressively assimilated
> into middle class society has been most frequently -
> and most persuasively - related to changes that have
> had their effect chiefly in out-of-work life...it is as
> a consumer and householder, as a family man and member
> of the local community that he ceases to be
> recognizably different from his white-collar neighbours
> and fellow citizens (1969:85).

A sample of men, blue collar and some white collar, were

interviewed at work and again at home with their wives. The

neighborhoods in which their homes were located varied in

status, including some with a mixed class composition and

others that were more homogeneous.

In many respects the data corroborated that of the

studies cited above on new towns and housing estates.

Contacts with kin are equally infrequent among both social

classes (1969:88). The home takes on increasing importance

in a variety of ways as a setting for joint husband and wife

activity. Husbands devote their leisure time to repairs

within the home, working in the garden, and assisting their

wives with selected domestic chores. A similar pattern was

found among the white collar workers in the sample.

> ...it would appear that while our affluent workers are,
> as husbands, as family centered as the white-collar
> workers we studied, the white-collar workers are on a
> number of counts little or no less privatised in their
> social life than are our affluent workers and their
> wives [Goldthorpe et al 1969:92].

Status buying prevails in both classes. In short, there

is a common tendency to derive nearly all social

satisfactions from home and family, in this case meaning the

nuclear family.

Yet major differences still divide the two class samples.

Wider social contacts are not pursued in the same manner.

While the affluent workers count their friends principally

among neighbors and kin, in the white collar sample friends

are drawn far more from other categories, including

workmates. Possibly of the greatest importance is the

finding that the middle class couples rely more heavily on

joint activities and share more mutual social contacts than

do the manual couples. Entertaining in the home follows

differing patterns as well.

> Further analysis of the data in fact reveals that as
> many as 42% of the manual couples (compared with 24% of
> the white-collar sample) reported entertaining at home
> only couples who were kin - if indeed they
> 'entertained' at all - and that another 33% mentioned
> no more than one couple apart from kin whom they would
> meet in this way...social occasions of the kind in
> question were not, in the main, particularly frequent
> occurrences in these respondents' social lives - taking
> place on average somewhat less than once a month
> [Goldthorpe et al 1969:92].

The manual couples are also less involved in formal
associations other than trade unions and work (factory)
clubs. Added to the information on general sociability, it
would seem that while a common marked degree of privatization
exists, the traditional class differences in life styles
still come through. The relative tendency of husbands and
wives in the blue collar sample to segregate their social
contacts carries forward an old pattern, that is the division
between his "mates" and her relatives, adjustments to the new
environment notwithstanding.

Goldthorpe et al make a point of examining the status
aspirations of their informants (1969:116-156). Although
they agree that the affluent workers often fall into a
pattern of buying for the home, sometimes at considerable
sacrifice, their aspirations differ from those of what they
understand to be the typical middle class model, that is, a
climb up the a ladder of progressively higher statuses. The
manual worker respondents were not much oriented toward this
particular model of society and concept of advancement.
While they value higher pay, education for their children and
the acquisition of material goods, these are more means
toward a comfortable existence than status symbols.

These authors conclude that a lot of surface adoption by
blue collar workers of middle class culture has been read as
proof of incipient embourgeoisement when closer examination
reveals no underlying structural convergence. On the whole

their arguments are well documented; little suggest that the manual workers' life styles are becoming middle class on any more than a superficial level.

There is, on the other hand, a separate but related thesis that is not so readily refuted, that certain sectors of the middle and working classes, in particular those with similar incomes, are evolving their life styles in a single new direction. In the Luton sample, the white collar respondents as a group tend to fall wide of the stereotype of the middle class, so that while measurably different from the working class sample, they are not enough so to seem quite truly middle class. Above all, there is the manifestation of "privatization" in both class samples, the acting out of home and public life within a restricted network of social interaction.

> There is here, then, some possible support for the idea that we previously advanced of a process of 'normative convergence' between affluent manual and lower-level white-collar groups - one focal point of this being an overriding concern with the economic fortunes and social relationships of the conjugal unit...a majority of our manual and white-collar couples do have in common a propensity to devote their spare time overwhelmingly to home and family and to limit their wider social contacts even to the point at which the family is in near isolation.

> How far and in what ways this might represent a new pattern of white-collar sociability is diffficult to say for want of comparative material [Goldthorpe et al 1969:107-108].

The authors go on to note that class "patterns of sociability" are still distinct. The "want of comparative

material" has since been slightly alleviated, enough to
suggest that changes in socializing habits among Luton's
white collar workers may be more apparent than real.

In describing the middle class of a Swansea estate, Bell
(1968) found a distinction useful between "spiralists" and
"burgesses." Spiralists are geographically and socially
mobile, their ambitions tuned towards career advancement.
Burgesses are have deeper roots in the community, and, while
they accept in principle the ideal of career advancement,
their greater orientation towards the community makes work
more a means of supporting them in that role than an absolute
measure of status. The burgesses maintain extended family
ties, and use these ties in a manner very much like the
members of established working class communities, though the
extended family structures are not necessarily the same. The
spiralists, more than the burgesses, have extensive networks
of social relations with colleagues and means of making
friends in new contexts.

What happens to burgesses who find themselves removed to
new surroundings away from their old ties? If they do not
readily adopt spiralist goals and habits, they might quite
plausibly become privatized, in much the same manner as the
affluent manual workers and for much the same reasons, a
convergence of forms due to common experience with a new
environment. The Luton white collar workers were of the
lower echelons, not in management capacities, and in general

unlikely candidates for major advancement. Their privatized
habits thus appear explicable without reference to a
nationwide pattern of class convergence.

Much needs to be done in the way of studies of the middle
class. Bell notes the dearth of information on
intergenerational mobility in many studies, including his on
Swansea. One must also suspect - and it is occasionally
admitted - that the writers on the working class, most of
them of middle class backgrounds (with some exceptions,
notably Hoggart [1957] and Jackson [1968]), rely heavily on
their own experiences, and one would expect academic
sociologists to be spiralists. One lesson of the Swansea
study is that one sector of the middle class is not quite so
distant from working class habits as has been generalized.
Convergence is all too easily misread when members of that
sector share a common experience with blue collar workers.

Evidence abounds that fundamental differences in social
ideology persist long after common environmental experiences
have produced a convergence of forms. The Luton findings,
the various community studies on the working class, Hoggart's
(1957) remembrances, and the few pertinent studies of the
middle class (Bell, 1968; Firth, Hubert, and Forge 1970)
point to deep seated contrasts in social aspirations and
alignments, reflecting patterns that might well persist
through some common experiences. The oldest council housing
estates and "new" towns now afford the opportunity to view a

generation that has grown up there, a generation that could
again cultivate older forms of social networks.

Willmott's The Evolution of a Community: A Study of
Dagenham after Forty Years (1963) proves to be a more
critical test than the Luton study of some parts of the
embourgeoisement thesis. Dagenham is a vast estate of 27,000
homes established by the London County Council during the
early 1920's. The study attempts a reconstruction of the
early years of the estate and a comparison of social forms of
that time with four decades later.

Drawing largely on the memories of older informants,
Willmott concludes that Dagenham's social life in the early
years followed the pattern noted for new housing areas. The
residents were overwhelmingly working class, drawn from all
over Great Britain, but above all London's East End. Most
residents' ties with relatives in the old community became
attenuated, women's contacts with "mum" reduced to visits on
special occasions. In many households the women saw their
parents less often than the husbands saw theirs, especially
if work brought the men back to their old London
neighborhoods. Privatization describes the pattern very
well, though Willmott does not use the term.

Many of the estate's houses were distant from the few
neighborhood conveniences, including the three pubs (one for
every 9,000 people, less than a tenth the national average at
the time). Leisure time was spent in the home. Clubs and

societies never flourished. Working in the garden became a

major male activity, along with devoting time to the family.

Visits among neighbors were few, and informants recalled

neighbors'aloofness and rivalries sometimes expressed in the

form of competitive status buying. The turnover of residents

was high, many becoming quickly disillusioned and moving out.

Contemporary published accounts (Mass-Observation 1943; T.

Young 1934) bear out what informants remembered, that

community life was far from satisfying. People who stayed

did so because of the material advantages, not because they

found an environment into which they fit comfortably.

Some aspects of privatization have persisted with the

passage of time. Pubs and shops still have limited social

functions. Men spend more time in the home than their

counterparts in older working class neighborhoods. But these

phenomena appear to be dictates of the physical environment,

not fundamental redirections of social interaction, because

the traditional working class social system has been

reconstituted in most other respects.

> Throughout this book Dagenham has been compared with
> the 'traditional' working-class community. At the end,
> one is impressed by how similar, not how different,
> they are. Local extended families, which hold such a
> central place in the older districts, have grown up in
> almost identical form on the estate, and so have local
> networks of neighbours - people living in the same
> street who help each other, mix together and are on
> easy-going terms. In people's social status and class,
> their political loyalties, again, there are close
> parallels between the two districts. In part, Dagenham
> is the East End reborn (Willmott 1963:109).

The kinship system resumed its traditional form and role as a generation grew up on the estate. Mothers and daughters renewed their ties, and "mum's" home became once again the social center for her daughters. Matrilocality is now nearly as pronounced as in Bethnal Green, despite the Council's policy of giving priority to new migrants from London's more dilapidated sections when houses are assigned.

Neighbors visit one another in their homes, much more so than in the East End, but alternative places to socialize are scarce. What is noteworthy is that friends are recruited from the neighborhood, not among workmates, fellow members of voluntary associations, or other sources featured in the embourgeoisement argument.

Dagenham's pubs were subject to the same kind of social engineering that the whole estate reflects, and the history of their use brings us back to a point at which pub trends can be related to the theses of privatization and class convergence. Social planners of the 1920's viewed Dagenham among other things as a place where the pub would lose its traditional place and become the ostensibly healthy, family oriented establishment so favored by "improvement" enthusiasts. Dagenham pubs are very much on the "improved" model, very large and built according to those tenets.

If the purpose of "improvement" was simply to promote temperance, Dagenham's planners achieved some lasting success. Only 21% of the adults in the Dagenham sample had

been to a pub in the month prior to their being interviewed
(Willmott 1963:87). The dispersal of the pubs must be a
major reason; it would be interesting to know how car
ownership and the distance of homes from pubs affect
attendance, but these data are not reported. Yet another
reason for the poor attendance is the low regard of residents
for the pubs.

> 'They did it all wrong when they built those places'
> said Mr. Kemp. 'Instead of little pubs that could be
> like little clubs for the people round about, like they
> are in Poplar, they built them whacking big places.'
>
> 'The public houses in Bethnal Green where we used to
> live were very friendly, small places. When you went
> up to the bar you said, 'Good evening, Fred, the
> usual,'and you got a 'Good evening' reply. But round
> here you lose the personal touch as far as the pub is
> concerned. You're just a customer in a big store, sort
> of thing. They accomodate more people than the pubs in
> Bethnal Green, and naturally the fewer people there are
> in a public house the more you know, the more there are
> the fewer you know' (Willmott 1963:87-88).

Those responsible for allocating and designing Dagenham's
pubs were far out of step with public wants, and in fact took
upon themselves the right to reshape those wants. In many
parts of England, and especially in later decades, estates
have had better access to pubs, designs have been more
moderate and sympathetic, and, as noted in earlier chapters,
traditional use of pubs has been kept or restored. Whereas
in Dagenham my own brief observations showed an unusually
high proportion of young pubgoers and a heavy emphasis in
design and promotion on the youth system, often the case in
leftover "improved" pubs. The expressed nostalgia of

Dagenham's residents for the older, cozier type of house
shows that the planners never succeeded in eradicating
expectations geared to well rooted patterns of pub use and
social participation. Dagenham's pubs reflect the community;
privatization is partial, enforced by outside agencies, and
not a sign of working class embourgeoisement.

To back away from this extreme case, a lesser degree of
class convergence might be read in other, more general
trends. Changing public demand is one cause of license
reduction, along with new demands of managemnt and the
policies of the licensing authorities. Casual entertainment
is increasingly a function of pubs, and together with the
growth of the youth and bistro systems might be taken to
indicate at least a partial shift to a new life cycle of pub
use, one shared by working class and middle class adults
alike. Young adults would combine participation in small
groups with highly mobile habits and a preference for large,
highly public lounges, while older, married couples would
retreat to the socially restricted confines of the bistro
system. Evidence of privatization might also be found in the
large increase in home consumption of alcoholic beverages.
But this scenario too proves to be exagerrated.

Changes in the Pubs: Form, Content, and Meaning

Given that the short supply of pubs on estates built
during the interwars years contributed to a kind of

situational privatization, but that the relatively small
housing estates of Bolton and Fenston do not greatly disturb
pubghoing habits, it was deemed worth some effort to observe
a large public housing estate whose residents have at hand a
wide selection of accessible pubs. One Huntingdon pub, on
such an estate, was observed for a week. Designed to
accomodate varied use, it has cozy alcoves in the lounge and
the "Public Bar," and the usual pub games are much in
evidence. Social, thrift, and sick clubs operate. The
regulars' system thrives, utilizing the whole of the pub at
times, often alongside other uses. Yet though the pub was
expressly built to accomodate a variety of neighborhood
users, is well thought of by its patrons, and is a local to
many of them, most of the regulars frequently drive, bus, or
walk the nearly two miles to the older pubs in the center of
the town, acting much like the mobile regulars of Bolton.

Postmortems on old pubs and old pubgoers, this report has
repeatedly noted, are premature, and nothing in the mere fact
of having a new home with a garden on a long term lease will
by itself cause the inhabitants to change their pubgoing
habits. The feeling that it should is a hangover from the
temperance movement, based on the perception of the pub as a
social pathology fed by the refugees of shattered homes.
Such notions were expressed best in the "improved public
house" movement and the vast interwar estates, but are not
entirely dead. Change could still be forced, people

relocated to St. Kilda and all beer stopped at the water's
edge. Yet the Luton and Dagenham studies reveal the
resilience of social formations, and my own data find new
estates and older forms of pub use perfectly compatible,
given the opportunity.

The regulars not only carry on, they continue to recruit
new members. Most youthful pubgoers are adept at
participating in diverse systems. Pub use is thereby
becoming, if anything, more varied where a variety of pub
environments is available. In some of those few places where
settings are reduced to a small, look alike assortment of
lounges - Dagenham was the prototype - use is perhaps
becoming less varied, and either that or the impersonal
effect of design and management discourage patronage. But
given half a chance, through creative design or favorable
management policies, the regulars carve out a niche within
settings whose original inspiration was a movement that would
have sent them all home.

Because pubgoers are so adept at different uses of pubs,
systems compete not for souls but merely for attention.
Unless this is understood, it is all too easy to misread a
diversification of old habits as the replacement of old ones.
Privatization, as it may or may not be manifest in the pubs,
is relative. The bistro system represents a wholesale
privatization of pub use only where enforced changes in pub
availability and design make it so, and the youth system is

not quite so private under any circumstances. Pubs are no
longer community centers, but Bolton and Fenston pubgoers
retain networks of pub contacts, and so presumably would many
more Dagenham residents if they had the chance.

Class convergence too can be too read too easily, and
wrongly, in changing habits of using pubs, particularly the
end of whatever segregation by class was once found among pub
rooms, and in the diminution of many class-associated
preferences in drinks and other features. But the odd ones
in the prewar pubgoing mix were those who preferred
gentlemen's drinking rooms and the cocktail bars of bonafide
hotels. Many middle class patrons, probably Bell's
burgesses, all along had local ties and participated in a
manner hardly distinguishable from working class patrons.
The end of class segregation means simply the near end of a
dissenting tradition, and if some middle class patrons are
especially prone to act on more widely shared preferences for
archaic architectural styles, young Etonians may also be seen
rubbing elbows in some public bars these days. To the degree
that class convergence is acted out in the pubs, there is
more proletarianization of the former dissenters than
embourgeoisement of anyone else.

Cars, Television, and Pubs

Two innovations, television and car ownership, are often
credited with or blamed for a great effect on pubs. Both

developments obviously figure in any complete discussion of
privatization. It is therefore apropos to assess the exact
impact on the pubs.

Commentators quite frequently make television the prime
cause of increasing home sales of beer, a lure that draws
people away from pubs. The thesis is logical, and an
association between television and off-licence is evident in
Table III. If television is a source of entertainment, then
it is competing with the pubs in the very function being most
vigorously developed. Television could thus be both a
contribution to privatization and a competitor for the
attention of those married couples that are at the heart of
the whole sociological debate.

On the other hand, the spread of home television is too
much intertwined with other factors for the relevant
statistics to be conclusive. Television cannot readily be
identified from nationwide statistics alone as the cause of
growing off-license sales, in part because the spread of
television has been so gradual. The statistics for retail
beverage sales and television license issue are not compiled
for the same districts, making a more meaningful breakdown
hard to achieve.

Informants in this study generally felt that elderly
pubgoers who would once have gone to a pub now often stay
home nights and watch television. Otherwise, most informants
did not feel television has a great impact. Several did

TABLE III

Television Licenses and Off-Licenses

in England and Wales

Year	Television licenses	Justices' off-licenses
1920	—	22,198
1940	—	21,884
1945	—	21,559*
1950	343,882	23,532*
1955	4,503,766	23,914*
1960	10,469,753	23,670
1962	11,833,712	24,644
1964	12,885,331	25,838
1966	13,567,090	26,590

* includes suspended licenses

offer that people owning sets for the first time often stayed glued to them, but that this habit passes with time. Cauter and Downham (1954:159) found television ownership has a slight but significant negative effect on pubgoing, but television was then still very much a novelty. Recent indications are that television viewing may have peaked in most of the countries where it came earliest. The future prospects of the pubs, all things considered, are in no apparent danger from this source.

Car ownership has spread rapidly over the past two decades, except in the poorest sectors of the working class. A car is a prime status symbol wherever status buying has developed, and among the Luton workers car owners were found to be slightly more home oriented. But no one has yet argued that car ownership causes privatization or alters fundamental social alignments, and the Fenston and Bolton findings seem to show little such effect. As noted in the preceding chapter, car owners range further on casual pub visits, but their loyalty to a local is unchanged. Even the young follow their parents' choices in locals.

The breathalyzer test, used by police to measure drivers' blood alcohol, is thought by many to discourage pubgoing. Publicans' opinions vary greatly. Pub sales dipped slightly the year the breathalyzer was put into use, then recovered. Long term effects are again lost among all factors affecting the trade, but national statistics do not indicate the breathalyzer has had a drastic, lasting effect. The majority

of pubgoers still travel on foot. Men of average size pass

the breathalyzer test after they have consumed a pint of

bitter, two pints if they spread them over about an hour and

a half. The typical casual visit does not involve more than

this, and one's local is usually a place to which one does

not need to drive. In areas where the pub supply is thinning

out, and application of the drunk driving law is strict, it

might well be expected that wandering between pubs would be

curtailed, but my data are insufficient to permit any

judgement. Finally some heavy drinkers, especially young

ones, ignore the law completely.

The test has had a marked effect in certain situations.

In particular, trade has fallen off at those pubs near mills

that rely heavily on a lunch hour and after work trade from

workmen. Such pubs in Fenston, Bolton, Manchester and

Newcastle-upon-Tyne were found to have almost without

exception lost trade steadily in the postwar years, and at an

especially rapid rate after the introduction of the

breathalyzer. Informants were found at other pubs who used

to drop in at quitting time to places nearer work, but

frequently gave the test as the reason they had stopped.

Brewery representatives were unanimous that these particular

pubs have become poorer prospects, but that otherwise the

law's impact has not been great.

Non-alcoholic or low alcohol drinks, sometimes touted as the way to have pubs and sober driving too, are not all that much in evidence in pubs. They are consumed mostly by women accompanying men, and in these cases the beer drinker still usually ends up the driver. Shandies (a mixture of one half beer and one half lemonade) and "Bloody Barbaras" (straight tomato juice, named after Barbara Castle, the Member of Parliament who authored the breathalyzer bill) have never really caught on with males. Though soft drinks are actually more profitable for the publican than beer, many landlords remain very negative about men who come in and consume nonalcoholic beverages. Obviously, the publican is giving priority to traditional ideas of what a pub is for.

QUENCHING THE BROILERHOUSE

Patrick Goldring's essay, The Broilerhouse Society (1969), likens modern mass society, specifically England, to a broilerhouse in which hens are maintained in batteries of cubicles, their feed, excrement, background music and other stimuli monitored by computer. The metaphor is a bit severe, perhaps, but the author does raise a valid question whether the concentration of social life in the home is creating a monotonous, lifeless society.

> Broilerhouse culture begins at home and as far as
> possible stays there. If the human broilerhouse is to
> operate with maximum efficiency, it is necessary to
> keep people as far as possible at home or at any rate
> in their own immediate neighorhood [Goldring 1969:63].

Goldring views pubs, and all drinking, as enemies of the broilerhouse.

> ...it soon becomes clear that alcoholic drink has no real place in a broilerhouse society and is on the way out, however slowly. For centuries past, we have been drinking to become cheerful to forget troubles and to drop our inhibitions. In the course of seeking these reliefs we have also become incoherent, disorganized, violent, unpredictable and uncontrollable - none of which states is appropriate to broilerhouse life [1969:92-93].

> ...some council estates have provided pubs which have done a roaring trade but the roaring has most often been done by young people in pre-broilerhouse freedom, attracted by jazz or pop groups, rather than by serious drinkers. There has been some increase in wives taking a drink with their husbands, but perhaps because the pub is now losing some of its traditional attraction for husbands. It is also transforming itself from a drinking to an eating-and-drinking-and-entertainment place. Eventually it will cease to be a pub, which has no real broilerhouse function [1969:95-96].

In comparison with this report, Goldring identifies the same trends in pubs, but finds them proceeding more quickly and more surely to completion, a difference of perspectives which may depend on one's time scale. Nearly all present day pubs might well appear to be broilerhouse institutions if compared to the tight little neighborhood alehouses of past centuries. But if "traditional" refers to pubs before the last world war, the contrast does not appear nearly so great, and neither a loss of all traditional use nor a total stereotyping of pubs seem so certain prospects for the foreseeable future.

Pubs have individual character despite conventions that signal types of pubs and appropriate uses of those pubs, but

advertising, urban planning and centralized ownership could
reduce their variety. The argument that planners only give
people what they want commits the fallacy of confounding the
general with the particular. If one were to collect
everyone's preferences in pubs; what lighting, floor plan,
services and whatever else are most preferred; and embody
them all in one pub, there would simply be one more pub, not
one to suit everyone. The dangers of applying singular
marketing criteria and standards of efficiency lie not in the
elimination of pubs but in the building of optimum pubs: the
most popular, the most profitable, the healthiest, etc. This
sort of triumph has always been attempted on a local scale,
the "finest on the street," but to build a type of pub around
the country because it has proven popularity would be another
matter. Though I have classified pubs and parts of pubs, I
must add that tradition rests to no small degree on
idiosyncratic expression in design and use.

Traditional pub culture is more remarkable for its
resilience and adaptability than for its pliability in the
hands of would-be social engineers. New users are carving
out their own traditions. Rather than restrict choice by
trying to find a few best pub designs and tailoring
managerial policies to a similar optimum, the strategy most
apt to suit everyone would be to supply a number of pubs of
such a size as is practicable and to use enough imagination
in design and managerial policy to permit ongoing evolution

of each individual house. Bold underplanning may well be the
best way to keep the pubs that we have known.

In fact rigidly stereotyped pubs do not loom so large as
critics would have it. The most hidebound concepts of a pub
belong not to the present but to the improved public house
movement. During the postwar period of renovation, some
monotonously similar lounges certainly emerged, but as
construction and recontruction have gone ahead, so too have
the breweries, individual owners, and other influential
parties begun to show more flexibility. I would not yet go
so far as to say that bold underplanning is the rule, but
some modest moves in that direction may be detected.

These signs, favorable to those who would conserve the
institution, reflect a probable limit to the changes that
worry those same observers, and not an immediate halt to the
trends. Unless and until bold underplanning is sufficiently
in place to balance the effects of license reduction, a
danger remains that much variety will be sacrificed to the
objective of catering to narrow, normative concepts of public
demand. It is entirely conceivable that in time the majority
of pubgoers will have experienced the loss of their favorite
pub, or a part thereof, because someone thought, rightly or
wrongly, that it appealed to too narrow a range of patrons.

The lesson is one that might be applied to the whole
broilerhouse argument. The majority are noncomformists in
some way, and that may rescue us from the imposition of utter

conformity, but some amount of presently existing local variation is sure to be lost.

Number of Pubs in England and Wales
and Their Ratio to Population

Year	Number of Licensed Premises	Persons/License
1977[1]	about 25,000	200
1840[2]	100,640	158
1869[2]	122,420	291
1895[3]	103,341	387
1910[3]	92,484	387
1920[3]	83,432	451
1930[3]	77,821	509
1940[4]	73,365	544
1950[4] (includes suspended licenses)	73,483	596
1955[4] "	72,658	612
1960[4] (excludes suspended licenses)	69,184	661
1962[4] "	72,000	648
1964[4] "	74,012	641
1966[4] "	75,544	637

1. Medlik (1961:131) bases this estimate of English premises on the general enquiry of 1577, which excluded London and some other districts. Many authorities feel the count is low.

2. This is the number of "publicans" given in the Report of the Royal Commissioner of Interna; Revenue (1862:44).

3. Licensing Statistics 1921 and 1938.

4. Monckton 1969:162.

APPENDIX TWO

Pubgoers' Questionnaire

Sampling Method

Sampling and interviewing were carried out beginning at a peak evening hour in all pubs of the primary sample. On two nights the following questions were asked of the first three patrons to enter the pub. Socially separate rooms were treated as separate pubs.

Schedule

At which pub or pubs, if any, are you a regular? (This quesion often had to be rephrased, "Which pubs do you regularly visit?"

How often do you visit that (those) pub(s)?

What other pubs do you visit? How often?

Do you ever meet friends outside of the pubs before pubgoing? Where and how often? Do you travel with friends from pub to pub? Under what circumstances?

Where do you live? How often do you walk to a pub? Go by bus? Ride? Do you own a car? Do you drive it to pubs? Which ones? How often?

Do you belong to any pub teams and/or clubs? Which ones? Have you traveled with these groups in the past year? To where? Have you participated in pay out nights and other social parties?

APPENDIX THREE: A GLOSSARY OF PUB TERMS

<u>General</u>:

ale: the common type of English beer, made with fast
            fermenting yeasts and, unlike lager, not aged at
            low temperatures.

bar: a licensed room in a pub.

bar counter:

    a counter across which drinks are served, corresponding to
    one meaning of the North American <u>bar</u>.

beer: in the industry all fermented malt beverages, in
        Great Britain more commonly applied to ale than to
        lager, and in the United States to lager rather than
        ale.

best: denotes a better provided room or section of a pub,
        in which slightly higher prices are charged for
        drinks.

bitter: draught ale of medium alcoholic content, named for
        the slightly bitter taste imparted by an extra
        measure of hops. In 1969-70 the most popular beer
        sold in pubs.

cellar: the place where barrels of draught beer are kept,
        often but not always under the main rooms.

cellar temperature:

    in general what the name implies: the temperature of beer
    drawn from barrels in the cellar, but breweries now
    recommend refrigeration if necessary to maintain 55-60
    degrees F. for ale, lower for lager.

free house:
    a pub owned by someone other than a brewery, usually its
    operator.

keg beer: beer much like bitter, except that it is
                   pasteurized or sterile-filtered and packed under
                   compressed carbon dioxide gas. A better
                   standardized and slightly more expensive than
                   bitter, and a fast-growing item in 1969-70, but
                   criticized by many as lacking the flavor of the
                   true draught product.

lager: beer brewed with a particular strain of yeasts, and,
         if made in the traditional continental European
         fashion, aged for some weeks at low temperature.

landlord: commonly any publican, but in some places   only
             tenants and owners of free houses.

local: a pub that one frequents most often, typically close
         at hand, and often the pub where one is a regular.

manager: in the trade a person hired and paid a salary to
             operate a pub for its owner, nearly always a
             brewery.

mild: the lowest priced and least alcoholic (about 3% in
         most brands) draught ale. In the North many
         breweries market both "mild" and "best mild," the
         latter a slightly stronger brew that sells for about
         the same price as bitter, but like mild, has less hop
         taste than bitter.

regular: a person, usually but not always male, well
             known in a particular pub, and an active enough
             participant to be granted special recognition.

shandy: a half and half mixture of beer and "lemonade" (lemon
         soda in North America).

tenant: a publican who rents a tied house under contract with
         the brewer-owner.

tied house:

   a pub owned by a brewery, and let under a contract which
   specifies that the brewer's beer will be sold, along with
   soft drinks, wine and spirits that may be supplied through
   the brewery and sometimes a restricted number of specialty
   beers from other breweries.

Specific Names and Titles of Pub Rooms

As much as possible, the following approximate the meanings
of titles as they were originally applied to specific rooms
within pubs. The titles often remain on the door long after
the room changes in some way, and meanings also vary when
used by patrons generically or to refer to untitled rooms.
Many are subject to regional and local variation.

cocktail bar:

> originally a room in the best section, often one with a
> predominantly middle class clientele, but now often a small
> to medium-sized lounge with the highest price scale in the
> pub.

gentlemen's room:

> no longer heard or seen, and never to my knowledge a title
> on the door, but once used to refer to rooms where working
> class patrons were not welcome.

jug and bottle:

> formerly a room where draught beer was sold in customers'
> containers, now often a relict title on the door of a small
> room.

ladies' room:

> a room in the best section designed primarily for use by
> women, though the title was not widely used (see parlour).

lounge or lounge bar:

> most consistently a room in the best section, today most
> often medium to large and approximating the design
> described in Chapter Three.

parlour: highly variable, name and title once often
             commonly applied to a room mainly for women, but
             now used for almost any room in best section.

public bar:

> strictly speaking the room in which the lowest prices are
> charged for drinks, often designed along the linesa of the
> "classic public bar" of Chapter Three.

saloon bar:

    mainly in southern England, a room in the best section,
formerly sometimes the title of a gentlemen's room, now
nearly always a room on the lounge pattern.

snug: a small room either in the best section or off the
        public bar, now rare.

tap room: highly variable, but often a small room in the
        best section.

vault: mainly from northern England, usually the public bar.

BIBLIOGRAPHY

Askwith, Lord

    1928   British Taverns: Their History and Laws.
              London: Routledge and Sons.

Bell, C.

    1968   Middle Class Families: Social and Geographical
              Mobility. London: London and Kegan Paul.

Besant, Sir Walter

    1902   London in the Eighteenth Century. London:
              Black.

    1904   London in the Time of the Tudors. London:
              Black.

Bott, E.

    1957   Family and Social Network: Roles, Norms and
              External Relationships in Ordinary Urban
              Families. London: Tavistock.

Bracey, H.E.

    1959   English Rural Life: Village Activities,
              Organisation and Institutions. London:
              Routledge and Kegan Paul.

British Broadcasting Company

    1968   Annual Reports and Accounts. Parliamentary
              Papers, vol. 20, Mmnd: 3779. London: Her
              Majesty's Stationery Office.

Carter, H.

    1918   Control of the Drink Trade: A Contribution to
              National Efficiency, 1915-1917. London:
              Longmans, Green and Company.

Carter, H.

    1933   The English Temperance Movement. London:
              Epworth.

Cauter, T., and J.S. Downham

    1954   The Communication of Ideas: A Study of
              Contemporary Influences on Urban Life. London:
              Chatto and Windus.

Cavan, S.

    1966   Liquor License: an Ethnography of Bar Behavior.
              Chicago: Aldine.

Coates, K., and R. Silburn

    1970   Poverty: the Forgotten Englishmen. Middlesex:
              Penguin.

Cooper, D.

    1970   The British Eating Out in Pubs. London:
              National Catering Inquiry.

Dennis, N., P. Henriques, and C. Slaughter

    1956   Coal is Our Life. London: Eyre and
              Spottiswoods.

Finn, T.

    1966   The Watney Book of Pub Games. London: Queen
              Anne.

Firth, R.W.

    1956   Two Studies of Kinship in London.

Firth, R.W., J. Hubert, and A. Forge

    1970   Families and Their Relative: Kinship in a
              Middle-Class Sector of London: an
              Anthropological Study. London: Routledge and
              Kegan Paul.

Flannery, K.V.

    1967   Culture history versus cultural Process: a
              debate in American archeology. Scientific
              American 217(2):119-122.

Geertz, C.

    1963   Agricultural Involution: the Process of
              Ecological Change in Indonesia. Berkeley:
              University of California Press.

George, N.D.

    1967   London Life in the Eighteenth Century. New
              York: Harper and Row.

Goffman, E.

    1959   The Presentation of Self in Everyday Life.
              New York: Doubleday.

Goldring, P.

    1969   The Broilerhouse Society. London: Leslie
              Frewin.

Goldthorpe, J.H., D. Lockwood, F. Bechofer, and J. Platt

    1969   The Affluent Worker in the Class Structure.
              Cambridge: Cambridge University Press.

Gorer, G.

    1955   Exploring English Character. London: Cresset

Gorham, M., and H. McG. Dunnett

    1950   Inside the Pub. London: Architectural Press.

Gourlay, W.

    1906   National Temperance: a Jubilee Biograph.
              London: Richard J. James.

Green, M., and T. White

    1968   Guide to London Pubs. London: Sphere Books.

Hall, B.T.

1922   Our Sixty Years: the Story of the Working Men's
         Club and Institute Union. London: Working
         Men's Club and Institute Union.

Hall, E.T.

1959   The Silent Language. New York: Doubleday.

1963   A system for the notation of proxemic behavior.
         American Anthropologist 65:1003-1026.

1966   The Hidden Dimension. Garden City: Doubleday.

1968   Proxemics. Current Anthropology 9:83-108.

Harrison, W.

1968   (orig. 1587) Description of England, edited by
         G. Edelen. Ithaca: Cornell University Press.

Hattox, R.S.

1985   Coffee and Coffeehouses: the Origins of a
         Social Beverage in the Medieval Near East.
         University of Washington Press, Seattle.

Hoggart, R.

1957   The Uses of Literacy. London: Chatto and
         Windus.

Homans, G.

1941   English Villagers of the Thirteenth Century.
         Cambridge: Harvard University Press.

Jackson, B.

1968   Working Class Community. London: Routledge and
         Kegan Paul.

Janes, H.H.

1963   The Red Barrel: a History of Watney Mann.
         London: J. Murray.

Jennings, H.

    1962   Societies in the Making. London: Routledge and
              Kegan Paul.

Kerr, M.

    1958   The People of Ship Street. London: Routledge
              and Kegan Paul.

Klein, J.

    1965   Samples from English Culture. London:
              Routledge and Kegan Paul.

Kuper, L. (ed.)

    1953   Living in Towns. London: Cresset.

Lennard, R.V.

    1959   Rural England, 1086-1135: a Study of Social and
              Agrarian Conditions. Oxford: Clarendon.

Licensing Statistics

    1921, 1938   London: British Sessional Papers, House
        of Commons.

Lockwood, D.

    1966   Sources of variation in working class images of
              society. Sociological Review 14:249-268.

McGill, A. (ed.)

    1969   Pub: a Celebration. Harlow: Longmans.

Mass-Observation

    1943   An Enquiry into People's Homes. London: J.
              Murray.

    1970   The Pub and the People. London: Seven Dials.

Matthias, P.

    1959   The brewing industry in England 1700-1830.
              Cambridge: Cambridge University Press.

Medlik, S.

   1961   The British Hotel and Catering Industry.
            London: Pitman and Sons.

Mogey, J.M.

   1956   Family and Neighbourhood. London: Clarendon.

Monckton, H.A.

   1966   A History of English Ale and Beer. London:
            Bodley Head.

   1968   A History of the English Public House. London:
            Bodley Head.

Monopolies Commission

   1969   Beer: a Report on the Supply of Beer. London:
            Her Majesty's Stationery Office.

Morgan, L.H.

   1965   (orig. 1881) Houses and House Life of the
            American Aborigines. University of Chicago
            Press, Chicago.

Morning Advertiser

   Published weekly by the Licensed Victuallers;
   Association, London.

Morris Committee on War Damaged Properties

   1943   Report. London: Her Majesty's Stationery
            Office.

National Board of Prices and Incomes

   1969   Beer Prices. London. Her Majesty's Stationery
            Office.

Norum, G., N. Russo, and R. Sommer

   1967   Seating patterns and group task. Psychology in
            the Schools 4:276-280.

Oliver, B.

    1934   The Modern Public House. London: Fellowship of
                  Freedom and Reform.

    1947   The Renaissance of the English Public House.
                  London: Faber and Faber.

Osmond, H.

    1959   The relationship between architect and
                  psychiatrist. In Psychiatric Architecture, C.
                  Goshen, ed., Washington, D.C.: American
                  Psychiatric Association.

Peel, C.S.

    1934   Homes and Habits in Early Victorian England,
                  1830-1865. London: Oxford University Press.

Pratt, E.A.

    1907   The Licensed Trade: an Independent Survey.
                  London: John Murray.

Rowntree, B. Seebohm

    1902   Poverty: a Study of Town Life. London:
                  Macmillan.

Royal Commissioner of Internal Revenue

    1862   Report. London: Her Majesty's Stationery
                  Office.

Rye, W.B. (ed.)

    1967   England as Seen by Foreigners in the Days of
                  Elizabeth and James I. London: Bentham.

Sommer, R.

    1959   Studies in personal space. Sociometry
                  22:247-260.

    1961   Leadership and group geography. Sociometry
                  24:99-110.

    1969   Personal Space: the Behavioral Basis of Design.
                  Englewood Cliffs: Prentice-Hall.

Strodtbeck, J.L., and L.H. Hook

    1961   The social dimensions of a twelve man jury
             table. Sociometry 24:397-415.

Svalastoga, K.

    1959   Prestige, Class and Mobility. Copenhagen:
             Gyldenhall.

Titmuss, R.

    1966   Income Distribution and Social change. London:
             Allen and Unwin.

Trevelyan, G.M.

    1949-52 Illustrated English Social History. London:
             Longmans and Green.

Vaizey, J.

    1960   The Brewing Industry, 1886-1951. London:
             Pitman.

Webb, B., and S. Webb

    1963   The History of Liquor Licensing, Principally
             from 1700-1830.

Whitbread Library

    1947   Your Local. London: Whitbread Library.

    1950.   Your Club. London: Whitbread Library.

Williams, E.E.

    1924   The New Public House. London: Chapman and Hall.

Williams, W.M.

    1963   A West Country Village: Ashworthy. London:
             Routledge and Kegan Paul.

Willmott, P.

    1963   The Evolution of a Community: a Study of
             Dagenham after Forty Years. London: Routledge
             and Kegan Paul.

Young, M., and P. Willmott

    1957   Family and Kinship in East London. Middlesex:
              Penguin.

    1960   Family and Class in a London Suburb. London:
              Routledge and Kegan Paul.

Young, T.

    1934   Becontree and Dagenham. Becontree; Social
              Service Committee.

Zweig, F.

    1952   The British Worker. Middlesex: Penguin.

    1961   The Worker in an Affluent Society. London:
              Heinemann.

INDEX